*Nā Mele*
*o*
*Hawai'i Nei*

# Nā Mele
## o
# Hawai'i Nei

### 101 HAWAIIAN SONGS

*collected by*

SAMUEL H. ELBERT *and* NOELANI MAHOE

UNIVERSITY OF HAWAII PRESS
HONOLULU

# CONTENTS

CHRISTMAS SONGS

# ACKNOWLEDGMENTS

The compilers wish to thank Wally Kuloloia, Bina Mossman, Mary Kawena Pukui, Koana Wilcox, and Ka'upena Wong for permitting their songs to be included.

University of Hawaii students provided an enthusiastic captive audience. Ka-ua-noe Kimura supplied much ethnological information and two extra stanzas to "Moana-lua"; Ruth Lei-lani Tyau's translations of " 'Auhea 'o ka Lani la," "Ho'oheno," and "Ku'u Ipo i ka He'e Pu'e One" seemed far superior to those of the instructor and she has kindly permitted their inclusion.

The manuscript was checked by that careful critic, Albert J. Schütz. We thank also Robert Hsu, who supervised the computer count of sound frequencies in Hawaiian, and Jean Charlot, our long-time friend, for the cover drawing.

Our deepest gratitude goes to Mary Kawena Pukui, the grandmother (Hawaiian fashion) of one of us, the co-worker of the other, and the true friend and inspiring teacher of us both. This book exists only because of her patient interpretations *o nā kau a kau* (from season to season).

Nā Mele
o
Hawai'i Nei

# INTRODUCTION

## SELECTION, CLASSIFICATION, AND ARRANGEMENT

These 101 songs are all postmissionary and owe their musical origin to missionary hymns. None of them are technically chants but some, such as " 'Ālika," "Hole Wai-mea," and "Maika'i Kaua'i," are chants that have been edited and set to music. The songs date from the mid-1850's to 1968—the date of Mary Kawena Pukui's Christmas song translations. The majority are from the time of the monarchy and so are already somewhat venerable. Nearly all are sung often today and are well known to Hawaiian singers. The texts have never before been written consistently with the glottal stops and macrons that make them nearly pronounceable by one not knowing Hawaiian. Many of them have not been translated before, or have been freely adapted rather than translated. Rarely have so many been assembled under one cover.

One aim of the selection was to include examples of the most common types of songs. The patriotic songs, such as "Hawai'i Pono'ī," are not sung at parties, nor are missionary temperance songs.

The songs are classified below according to dominant motif. This is sometimes difficult to assign because of a plurality of motifs in a single song. Most songs honoring places and ships, for example, have romantic connotations, as does the single war song.

| | | | |
|---|---|---|---|
| love songs, | 29 | songs about food, | 2 |
| songs honoring places, | 16 | children's songs, | 2 |
| songs honoring persons, | 12 | cowboy song, | 1 |
| songs about events, | 7 | genital song, | 1 |
| patriotic songs, | 5 | political song, | 1 |
| missionary and religious songs, | 5 | war song, | 1 |
| drinking songs, | 3 | dirge, | 1 |
| songs about ships, | 3 | Christmas songs, | 12 |

The love songs are perhaps unique in the world in several respects: their constant references to nature, their nearly constant happiness, and their anonymity and indirection. The most gifted composer of songs, especially love songs, was probably Queen Lili'u-o-ka-lani. Her "Puia ka Nahele," written in 1868, exemplifies the qualities named above. She sings of the distant uplands, the forest imbued with fragrance, wafted sweetness, infatuated birds, the sweet-eyed honey-eater, mist, rain creeping along a cliff, and ferns—no mention of a loved one, only a companion in the wet and misty forest, but we know that the fragrance and beauty are tributes to an unnamed love.

The following songs are classified as love songs:

"Adios ke Aloha"
"Ahi Wela"
" 'Ahulili"
"Alekoki"
"Aloha 'Oe"
"Hālona"
"Hi'ilawe"
"Ho'oheno"
"Ka-'ili-lau-o-ke-koa"
"Ka Makini Kā'ili Aloha"
"Ka Moa'e"
"Kāua i ka Huahua'i"
"Ka Ua Loku"
"Ke Ka'upu"
"Kokohi"

"Ku'u Ipo i ka He'e Pu'e One"
"Ku'u Pua i Paoa-ka-lani"
"Lei 'Awapuhi"
"Mai Hō'eu'eu Mai 'Oe"
"Manu 'Ō'ō"
"Pua Lilia"
"Puia ka Nahele"
"Pulupē Nei 'Ili i ke Anu"
"Puna Paia 'A'ala"
"Remember, Be Sure, and Be There"
"Sweet Lei Mamo"
"Wai o ke Aniani"
"Wai-pi'o"
"Wehiwehi 'Oe"

Songs honoring places may honor a single home (" 'Āina-Hau," "Ku'u Home o nā Pali Hāuliuli," "Old Plantation"), a valley, bay, or place ("Hanohano Hanalei," "Hilo March," "Kupa Landing," "Pūpū o 'Ewa"), a mountain ("Kilakila 'o Hale-a-ka-lā"), districts and a series of places ("Hilo Hanakahi," " 'Iniki Mālie," "Moana-lua," "Sassy"), or an island ("Ku'u Lei Pūpū," "Lāna'i," "Maika'i Kaua'i," "Moloka'i Nui a Hina").

Eight of the twelve songs honoring persons concern royalty. Those composed at a child's birth may be name songs (*mele inoa*) or genital songs (*mele ma'i*). Others composed later in the honoree's life may commemorate important events. The name songs for royalty in this collection are "He Inoa nō Ka-'iu-lani" and "He Inoa nō Kīna'u." The other songs honoring royalty are "A Kona Hema 'o ka Lani" (for Ka-lā-kaua), " 'Auhea 'o ka Lani la" (for Luna-lilo), "E Nihi ka Hele" (for Queen Ka-pi'o-lani when she left to attend Queen Victoria's jubilee), "Iā 'Oe e ka Lā (for Ka-lā-kaua starting out on his world tour), "Makalapua" (for Lili'u-o-ka-lani), and "Nā Hala o Naue" (for Queen Emma, composed after the death of her husband).

Emma De Fries honored a child ("Beautiful 'Ilima") and Lili'u-o-ka-lani sang of a perhaps imaginary grandmother in the early 1890's ("Tūtū"). Mary Kawena Pukui composed a name song in honor of her first grandson, La'akea, in 1949 ("Ku'u Lei"), and Ka'upena

Wong honored Alexander Spoehr (" 'Ālika Spoehr Hula") in 1961 when the latter left his position as director of the Bishop Museum.

Important events might be told in song, such as a trip to California ("Hele Au i Kaleponi"), an auto ride ("Holoholo Ka'a"), the installation of electricity ("Kāne'ohe"), the first water sprinkler ("Ka Wiliwiliwai"), a first moving picture ("Palisa"), a new hotel ("Royal Hawaiian Hotel"), a flight to the forest ("Pa'ahana"), a drunken spree ("Moana-lua"), or the annexation of Hawaii ("Kaulana nā Pua"). The last two have been classified with place songs and patriotic songs, respectively.

Two of the patriotic songs are responses to the feeling that every modern nation needed national anthems. In this category are "He Mele Lāhui Hawai'i" (by Lili'u-o-ka-lani) and "Hawai'i Pono'ī (by Ka-lā-kaua). Another, "Hawai'i Aloha" expresses Lorenzo Lyons's love for his adopted homeland. "Kaulana nā Pua," the only bitter song in this collection, was a plea to support Lili'u-o-ka-lani in her stand against annexation to the United States. The spirited and popular "Nā Ali'i" was an appeal by Samuel Kuahiwi to the Hawaiian societies to honor the departed chiefs, especially Kamehameha I.

The missionary and religious songs (other than Christmas songs) are "Ka Bana Kinai Rama" (temperance—or rather total abstinence), "Ku'u 'Īlio" (the badness of dogs), " 'Ekolu Mea Nui" (faith, hope, and aloha), "Queen's Prayer," and "Bili Boi" (which changed a charming and rather foolish love song to a plea to study books).

The drinking songs are "Kāmau Kī'aha," "Koni Au i ka Wai," and "Niu Haohao." The songs about ships are " 'Ālika," "Hula o Makee," and "Nā ka Pueo." The songs about food are "He 'Ono" and "Nā 'Ono o ka Āina." The children's selections, a new medium, are "Ke Ao Nani" and " 'Ekolu 'Iole Makapō." Single examples are given of cowboy songs ("Hawaiian Rough Riders"), genital songs ("Kō Ma'i Hō'eu'eu"), political songs ("Kamuela King"), war songs ("Hole Wai-mea"), and dirges ("He Kanikau nō Lele-iō-Hoku").

As to technical terms in Hawaiian for verbal arts, there was a paucity for types of prose and a plethora for types of poetry. The following is a summary of the most common types of verbal arts:

I. Types not repeated verbatim
   A. True or not true
       *mo'olelo:* story, tale, legend, myth, history, tradition, report, epic, narrative, fable, anecdote (also novel, romance, fiction, composition, article, journal, thesis, dissertation, monograph, book)
       *ha'i'ōlelo:* speech, oration, sermon, lecture

B.  Believed not true
   *ka'ao:* story, tale (novel, romance, fiction)
C.  Improvised chant: *paha, kepakepa*
II.  Types repeated verbatim
   A.  Spoken
      *'ōlelo no'eau:* proverb, epithet, motto
      *nane, 'ōlelo nane:* riddle, parable, allegory
   B.  Sung or chanted
      1.  For dancing
         *hula:* song, chant, dance
      2.  For dancing or not for dancing
         *mele:* song, chant, poem; some types of *mele: m. aupuni*
         (national anthem), *m. ho'oipoipo* (love song), *m. inoa*
         (name song), *m. ma'i* (genital song)
   C.  Sung only (and not for dancing)
      *hīmeni:* song
   D.  Chanted only (and not for dancing)
      General name: *oli*
      Classified according to theme:
         *kānaenae:* chant or prayer of eulogy
         *pule, kau:* prayer
         *kū'auhau, ko'ihonua:* genealogy
         *kanikau, kūmākena:* dirge, wail
      Classified according to manner:
         *kū'auhau, ko'ihonua:* genealogy
         *kepakepa:* rhythmic or conversational chant
         *kanikau, kūmākena:* dirge, wail
         *hō'aēaē:* chant with prolonged vowels
         *'i'i:* chant with deep rasping tremor
         *paha:* improvised chant
         (Many other kinds are listed in Pukui-Elbert, *English-
         Hawaiian Dictionary.*)

In summary, for the single Hawaiian prose term *mo'olelo,* there
are twenty-one English glosses, but for the single English term
"chant," some twenty-nine Hawaiian equivalents.

The term *hīmeni,* from English hymn, was introduced by the
missionaries, who did not want their hymns confused with pagan
*mele* and *oli.* Today any song not danced to is called *hīmeni,* and it
need not be religious. Songs and chants danced to are called hulas.

Roberts (1926:7) wrote that the modern music and the ancient
are as different "as it is possible for periods of the same art to be."
She was thinking of the musical aspects—so much more varied—
rather than the literary themes—so much less varied. The poetic
devices of modern and ancient forms remain rather similar.

6

In a study of the classification of the chants in the well-known legend of Kawelo (Elbert, 1959:32-113), Helen A. Topham listed vocative chants, chants of praise, chants of derision, boasts, descriptive chants, reminiscent or visionary chants, conversational chants, and religious incantations. Romantic chants are lacking, but they do occur in other legends, such as "Halemano" (Elbert, 1959:251-293), "Hiku," and "Kawelu" (Fornander, vol. 5:182-189). Proportionately, however, romance is highlighted more often in the songs than in the chants; could this be a form of acculturation to the Euro-American and Christian emphasis on romantic love? Of the chant types listed by Topham, the song types are rarely if ever derisive, boastful, visionary, conversational, or religious. The old gods Kū, Kāne, Kanaloa, and Lono, and the demigods Pele, Hi'iaka, and Kamapua'a, although prominent in the chants are rare in the songs. Is this due to the heavy hand of Christianity? Lamentations, also common in the chants, are not themes for song composers; one, Lili'u-o-ka-lani's dirge for her brother Lele-iō-Hoku, is included in this collection.

It has not been possible to include the melodies of the songs in this edition—a considerable task as many of the songs have never been transcribed in musical notation. Nor are the musical aspects of the songs discussed.

Barbara B. Smith (1959:52) characterized Hawaiian music as follows: "Old Hawaiian music has short regular phrases derived from hymn tune structure; simple harmonies suitable to the ukulele and guitar; melodic outlines based mostly on scale steps, skips with the basic chords, and lower-neighbor-note inflections; simple rhythmic patterns which are languidly performed; and a vocal style which may have been retained from ancient Hawaiian music, in which the singer slides from pitch to pitch."

In general, words in the songs are spelled as they are in the *Hawaiian-English Dictionary* (Pukui-Elbert, 1965) and *Place Names of Hawaii* (Pukui-Elbert, 1966). Words forming the name of a person are separated by hyphens. The glottal stops, carefully enunciated by Hawaiian singers, are indicated by a single quotation mark. Macrons, indicative of long vowels and stress, are marked except in positions in which the vowels are commonly sung short—this is a singer's privilege if the line is too long for the music.

Parenthetical phrases, as in "Adios ke Aloha" and "Pūpū o 'Ewa," indicate different parts, as male and female.

The songs are arranged alphabetically by the best-known title. The names of the composers and circumstances of composition, as well as poetic devices used, are noted wherever these are known.

As many stanzas as could be found are included, as well as variant lines. Formerly, there was as much interest in the words and the stories in these songs as there is, for example, in traditional Western American folk songs. Today the melody and the beauty of the dancers, rather than the story, are of paramount interest, and the words of some of the more recent songs not included in this collection are simple and artless.

## COMPOSERS

Of the eighty-nine traditional songs, 39 percent are anonymous. The known composers are listed in the Appendix, together with the titles of their compositions. Queen Lili'u-o-ka-lani with ten songs is by far the leader. Mary Kawena Pukui is second if one counts her three Christmas songs in addition to her two traditional songs. The composers still living are Kahale, Kuloloia, Mossman, Pukui, Wilcox, and Wong.

Lili'u-o-ka-lani, her brothers, Ka-lā-kaua and Lele-iō-Hoku, and her sister Likelike, are foremost among the composers. Beckwith (1919:311) stated "the arts of song and oratory, though practiced by all classes, were considered worthy to be perfected among the chiefs themselves and those who sought their patronage."

In some ways, poetry was aristocratic because the society was aristocratic. In ancient times high chiefs in Oceania and in Europe were considered divine, and it was a holy task to praise a lord; a difference in the Pacific is that members of the nobility themselves were at times creative and performing artists, rather than merely the sponsors of creation and performance. Chiefs received instruction in singing and dancing. One, Kawelo (Elbert, 1959:36-37), failed. Another, Halemano (Elbert, 1959:272-273), was told that the way to win back an unfaithful wife was not to fish and farm but to master song and dance; he did, and won her (but not forever). The legend contains his love chants, among the most beautiful in the language, but they do not reveal who composed them.

None of the Kamehamehas, except possibly Luna-lilo, were composers. The four siblings mentioned above excelled perhaps, as Roberts suggested (1926:8), because they were gifted and had "superior educational advantages."

Lili'u-o-ka-lani's notebook, in the State Archives, contains more than one hundred songs composed by her. Usually the melody is written by hand, the simple signature "Liliu," appears and sometimes the place and date of composition are given. English translations accompany some of the songs. Poetry and music afforded her solace during her many tribulations—her childlessness, the early deaths of so many close relatives, her own trial and imprisonment, and her unsuccessful efforts to regain her throne.

Perhaps equally gifted was her youngest brother, William Pitt Lele-iō-Hoku-ka-lā-hoʻolewa, who died in 1877 at the age of 22. He was born on the day of the funeral for Kamehameha III, and his name means "flight on the day of the full moon, the day of the funeral." He organized the famous Ka-wai-hau Glee Club. He is said to have composed a hundred songs during his short life—but where are they all?

Helen Caldwell (1915:78-79) has described a visit to Liliʻu about two years before her death:

"Queen Liliuokalani is well known as a modern Hawaiian composer. She lives quietly at Washington Place in Honolulu, and, though frail in health, at the age of 77 still takes much interest in the life of her people. In a visit to her home recently I found her seated between two royal *kahilis,* with her lap full of roses, which enhanced the beauty of her white hair and the simplicity of her black *holoku.* She was most gracious and told with animation of her love for music, of the inspiration a composer feels, and of the meles that were written in honor of her ancestors according to the ancient customs. It was a great honor she conferred in sending for one of her old retainers, who with the admirable dignity of carriage and manner characteristic of the Hawaiian matron, appeared at the doorway in an immaculate white holoku and yellow feather lei, the royal insignia, and chanted in weird and long-sustained tones one of the royal meles only heard on state occasions. As she chanted and portrayed with many gestures, the scenes described, the Queen explained the meaning thereof, and told how difficult of translation is the poetic thought embodied in the highly figurative language of the Hawaiians."

Many of the other composers were also musicians. Aeʻa, Ke-alakaʻi, and David Nape were in the Royal Hawaiian Band under the direction of Henry Berger. Heleluhe and Kong were with the Band later. Hiram Bingham and Lorenzo Lyons were missionaries, and Edward Kahale was for many years pastor at Ka-wai-a-Haʻo Church. Alohikea was a Kauai politician. Mary Kawena Pukui was for many years an associate in Hawaiian culture at the Bernice P. Bishop Museum. Bina Mossman was a sheriff, an active Republican, curator of the Queen Emma Home, and a leader of the Ka-ʻahu-manu Glee Club for many years. Kaʻupena Wong, the youngest of the composers, has won fame as a chanter and composer, and for his broad knowledge of Hawaiian culture.

# STRUCTURE OF THE HAWAIIAN LANGUAGE
## AND THE POETIC STYLE

Edward Sapir (1939:242) has pointed out that the major features of a literary style are given by the language itself. Can we say that the structure of Hawaiian in some way has influenced or even determined the stylistic forms of the poetry? For example, was the refusal to accept from the missionaries the device of rhyme in some way connected with the formal patterns of the language? Some of the grammatical features that may have reinforced stylistic aspects are listed below.

| Grammar | Poetic Style |
|---|---|
| (1) Small phonemic inventory<br>Reduplication<br>Invariable roots | Emphasis on repetition |
| (2) Focus on initials<br>Final whispering and loss of vowels | Lack of rhyme<br>Some irregularity in syllable count |
| (3) Nouns with no more than two qualifying content words<br>Noun phrases without verbs<br>Verb phrases without subjects | A staccato, terse effect<br>Catalogues of images, place names, and acts |
| (4) Lack of sexual gender<br>Near lack of tenses<br>Verbs without subjects<br>Verbless sentences | Ambiguity, vagueness, veiled and double meanings |

## Poetic Repetition

The distinctive sounds (phonemes) of Hawaiian are

p k ʻ h l m n w　　　( ʻ is a glottal stop)
i e a u o
ī ē ā ū ō　　(These vowels are long and always stressed)

Word stress is predictable, as in the following (　is primary stress, is secondary stress):

| | | | |
|---|---|---|---|
| páu | (finished) | wahī́ | (to wrap) |
| paʻū́ | (moist) | wahíne | (woman) |
| pāʻū́ | (sarong) | wāhíne | (women) |
| wáhi | (to split) | kàkahiáka | (morning) |

10

In connected discourse, according to a recent computer calculation, 60 percent of 3,347 successive sounds are vowels, 26.5 percent are *a* and *ā*, and 42 percent are *a, i,* and *k*. Thus there is not only a small inventory, but also a rather strong concentration in three of the eighteen possible sounds. One might also add that in spite of this meagerness allophones are few and include *v* as well as *w*, and a sound approaching the final vowel in *sofa* alternating with a sound like the *a* in Midwestern *father*.

A result of such a small selection of sounds is an abundance of homonyms and near homonyms, but instead of utilizing the latter for rhyme, they are enjoyed in puns and word play. A common pattern is repetition of the word (or word part) at the end of one line and at the beginning of the next. Roberts (1926:66) called this linked assonance. A more general term, linked terminals, is also applicable, as the terminals in the chants are frequently coupled antithetically as in the ancient creation chant, the *Kumulipo,* in which many fish are considered genetically related to plants with similar sounding names. In the following lines from the *Kumulipo* (Beckwith, 1951:line 239), the repetition is threefold.

| *Hānau* | *ka* | *'a'awa* | | *noho* | *i* | *kai* | |
| born | the | wrasse fish | | live | in | sea | |

| *Kia'i* | *'ia* | *e* | *ka* | *'awa* | *noho* | *i* | *uka* |
| guard | passive | by | the | kava | live | in | uplands |

The phonologically similar contrasting pairs are *kai/kia'i* and *'a'awa/'awa*. The pair with antithetical meanings is *kai/uka*. An informant reports that the *'a'awa* fish was used as a *pūpū* (relish) when drinking *'awa*.

Place names are commonly used in word play and echoism. Like other Oceanic peoples, the Hawaiians were constant name-givers and named not only land areas but also trees and rocks of legendary import, fishing grounds, and local winds, rains, and ocean currents. (One chant lists more than a hundred winds, including twelve in the single valley of Hālawa, Molokai (Fornander, vol. 5:103).

The names are largely understandable. *Place Names of Hawaii* (Pukui-Elbert, 1966) contains 1,125 entries, 88 percent of which have recognizable meanings. Some of the 12 percent without such meanings are ancient, such as Hawai'i, Moloka'i, and Kaua'i, and others have cognates elsewhere in the Pacific ('Upolu and Ka'ū on the island of Hawaii are cognate with 'Upolu and Ta'ū in Samoa); a few names have during the centuries been garbled beyond recognition. Place names have sentimental value to Hawaiians, their meanings are largely transparent, and they are therefore very prominent in songs and chants. Furthermore, their mastery is a witness of one's memory skills.

In three songs ("'Auhea 'o ka Lani la," "Kupa Landing," "Nā ka Pueo") lines ending with place names are followed in the next line by verbs. Thus linked are the places *Kai-mū, Ho'okena,* and *Māmala* and the verbs *ho'omū* (to crowd), *ho'oheno* (to cherish), and *mālama* (to protect).

The only recourse of a translator endeavoring to retain the word-play in English is to translate the place names with words echoing the translations of the verbs or, still harder, to find an English verb that echoes the Hawaiian place names—very difficult indeed if the English is not to sound absurd. In the first example the same morpheme *mū* occurs in both the name and the verb, and the place name might keep the assonance if it were translated "crowded sea," but people fond of the great surf at Kai-mū would not know that their favorite surf was heralded.

Repetition, so inevitable in a language with only eight consonants and ten vowels (half of which are long echoes of the other half), is further made structurally inevitable by the derivational feature of partial and complete reduplication, usually but by no means always indicative of plurality, repeated action, or continuous state. Here are some examples:

| Reduplications | | | | Song Name |
|---|---|---|---|---|
| *ho'ohiehie* to cherish | *ahiahi* evening | *lalawe* to overpower | *konikoni* palpitation | "Ahi Wela" |
| *mā'oki'oki* streaked | *hāwanawana* whispering | *Kīpu'upu'u* name of a rain | *'Apa'apa'a* name of a wind | "Hilo Hanakahi" |

Many common words, such as *ahiahi* (evening) and *ikaika* (strong), exist only as reduplications. Nearly every utterance and song of any length, then, will contain examples of this kind of repetition.

In the Christmas song "Kana Kaloka," note that of six content words in the first three lines of the third stanza, four of them are reduplications, so easy to learn and so pleasantly repetitive: *'olu'olu, 'umi'umi, pūhuluhulu, 'ula'ula.*

The invariability of content roots, a feature of the almost complete lack of inflections, may contribute to the effect of monotony, and the impression that the content roots have no alternate shapes other than those due to the changes of fast speech.

## Rhyme

With so many homonyms, rhyming would have been easy; it may be seen in the cruel missionary song "Ku'u 'Īlio." A hypothesis is offered here that rhyme may have been rejected because of the Hawaiian focus on initials. Alexander (1864:28) states: "The general principle of arrangement is that the emphatic word is to be placed at or near the beginning of the sentence." The usual sentence order is verb plus subject plus object (with the last two optional), and within the phrase the noun precedes the adjective. This order may be reversed, with these elements moved to the first and then brought into focus. Thus the second stanza of "Āina-Hau" begins

| Nā | ka | makani | aheahe | i | pā | mai |
|------|------|--------|--------|-----|------|--------|
| by | the | wind | gentle | did | blow | hither |

The wind (makani) is put first, in the emphatic position. The usual order would have been verb plus subject:

| Ua | pā | mai | ka | makani | aheahe |
|------|------|--------|------|--------|--------|
| did | blow | hither | the | wind | gentle |

Subtleties such as this are almost impossible to transmit through English. In this example, noun and qualifier could also be transposed to ke aheahe makani (the gentleness of the wind).

The use of place names illustrates the principle of focus. In "Hilo Hanakahi" and "Moana-lua," the places come first in the lines, and the less important poetic attributes and happenings follow. In "Hi'ilawe" the emphasis is on the girl's adventures and her beauty—the adventures and content words expressing beauty come first—rather than on the places Hi'ilawe and Wai-pi'o, which come at the ends of lines.

The suggestion is that with the poet's concentration on initial elements it seemed almost unnatural to worry about finals, and this unconcern may have been reinforced by the privilege of dropping or whispering vowels before pauses and even in the middle of utterances, particularly if the line seemed overly long to the chanter or singer. Even in conversation, vowels are devoiced or dropped in fast speech. Hele akula (go away) may come out hele kul. This freedom may have had the other effect of negating the necessity of exactness in syllable counts. If lines are too long, the chanter or singer may slur over some of the syllables.

## Terseness

In spite of an opulence of vocabulary with reference to nature, Hawaiian poetry in some ways seems terse, somewhat akin to

Chinese poetry, as described by Sapir (1939:243): "And Chinese, with its unmodified words and rigid sequences, has a compactness of phrase, a terse parallelism, and a silent suggestiveness that would be too tart, too mathematical, for the English genius." Whereas Hawaiian poetry could never be called "tart" it does have parallelism and balance and what Lorrin Andrews (1875:30), the first dictionary maker, called "terseness": "Hawaiian poetry for the most part consists of short, terse carefully adjusted sentences; all matter that can be is thrown out that the principal idea may make the stronger impression."

Roberts (1926:57) had a somewhat similar notion: "To the Hawaiian mind, the chief charm of the singing or chanting lay in the words, for their obvious meaning in many cases consisted of exquisite imagery, of word painting succeeding word painting, describing the beauties of natural scenery, used in a profusion bewildering to one accustomed to the restraints of most of our modern poetry."

Is grammar, and particularly syntax, related to terseness and successions of word paintings? What of the Hawaiian phrase versus the English phrase? Of the two, the Hawaiian phrase is apt to be the shorter, and the long, involved, entangled, embedded, bewildering-to-a-Polynesian phrases of English (such as this one) would be broken down into at least six phrases or clauses. Many Hawaiian phrases consist of a single content word and its optional accompanying particles that reveal grammatical relationships. If one calls the noun (N) or verb (V) and accompanying content words (C) the nucleus of the phrase, one may tally the types of nuclei in the most famous of Hawaiian songs, Queen Lili'u-o-ka-lani's "Aloha 'Oe," as follows:

| Nucleus | No. of Examples |
| --- | --- |
| V | 13 |
| V + C | 2 |
| N | 19 |
| N + C | 4 |
| N + C + C | 1 |

Thus about 82 percent of the nuclei in this song consist of a single content word (V or N), 15 percent of two content words, and 3 percent of three content words. In other words, 82 percent of the words are unmodified except by particles.

Another structural factor that may contribute to what Andrews has called terseness is the privilege of successions of noun phrases without verbs. "Hilo Hanakahi" consists of twenty-three noun phrases, naming in clockwise order important districts and places on the island of Hawaii. Each place name is followed by a phrase describing a natural attribute (rain, pandanus, wind, sea, and

14

cliffs), and all this is finally followed by a single verb. Certainly here is Roberts' succession of word paintings.

The lack of a verb "to be" and the sparseness of degrees of adjectives in Hawaiian were called by William Ellis (1826:339) "the greatest imperfections in the language." This lack may actually give a directness and vividness to the language, as in the following from the song "Toumi Toumi":

'O kou lei ia            your lei this
'O ua lei nei         aforementioned lei here

Terseness may be felt as a result of verbs without subjects, ungrammatical in English but commonplace in Hawaiian, as in the following literal translation of the Queen's song "Tūtū" about a forgetful grandmother:

> Coming to the evening,
> Preparing for devotion,
> Looking for glasses,
> Auwē! disappeared!
> There on the forehead,
> On the forehead placed,
> Quite forgotten,
> High on the forehead.

Beckwith, in her perceptive introduction to the long narrative "Laieikawai" (1919:295), said that in this work it was necessary to sacrifice what she in evolutional manner called "the brevity of primitive speech." This is true in narrative, as in English most sentences require verbs, and most declarative verbs require subjects, but in poetry one has more freedom, and lack of subjects or verbs need not jar (with an occasional judicious insertion of "to be") and may actually enhance effectiveness or impart freshness or boldness.

Need the wedding of terseness and repetition seem incongruous? Not necessarily. Repetition (other than that in reduplications) is commonly in different lines, and each line retains its simplicity. The simplicity may be what Roberts called "exquisite imagery" or what Colum described as "more imagistic than Amy Lowell" (quoted by Plews, 1968:178), but it is still laconic when compared with the involved sentences occurring in many other languages. Hawaiian poetry may consist of a string of pearls exquisite but separate, whereas in Euro-American poetry the pearls may be interlocked and entwined.

### Vagueness, Ambiguity, and Veiled Meanings

Cultural factors, such as the desire to be polite and the rudeness of direct requests for favors or blunt refusals to requests, should not

15

be considered in a discussion of veiled meanings. Yet the habit of being polite may have been carried over into song writing. It would never do, for example, to mention the real name of a sweetheart. The grammar, as pointed out, contributes to this vagueness—such things as verbless sentences and subjectless verbs. Two other structural factors may result in vagueness: the lack of explicit and obligatory sexual gender in many terms and the lack of any expression of tense in most sentences.

In English, words for sweetheart, friend, and companion are not inherently sex-explicit (they may be in other Indo-European languages), but the following are sex-linked in English but not in Hawaiian:

| English | Hawaiian |
| --- | --- |
| he, she | *ia* |
| brother, sister | *kaikua'ana, kaikaina* |
| she and I, he and I | *māua* |

It is sometimes hard to know whether ego and addressee in the songs are male or female. In "Hele Au i Kaleponi," the sex of the addressee is told only by the femininity of the clothes she demands. The song is completely without tense, and this must be supplied in English, in this case, present and past.

The *kaona,* or veiled meanings, in the songs are treated in a later section.

Most Christian names in European languages are sex-linked, but not so in Hawaiian. And almost any name consists of recognizable words. In the dirge "He Kanikau nō Lele-iō-Hoku," Ka-lā-kaua is called Ka-uli-lua, and Likelike is Ka-pili. *Ka-uli-lua* means "the double blackness," and *ka'ulī lua* is "creeping twice." *Ka pili* is "the relationship." One not knowing these special names for Ka-lā-kaua and Likelike could not understand or translate the song.

An ambiguity in the writing system—not in the language—makes the translator's task doubly difficult. This comes from the failure to indicate, in writing, glottal stops and long vowels. *Ko'u* (mine) and *kōu* (yours) may alike be written *kou.* *Ala* (road, awake), *'ala* (fragrance), and *'āla* (rock) are usually written *ala.*

## Summary

The translator of Hawaiian poetry who wants to impart a hint of the poetic structure of the original may endeavor to mirror the Hawaiian devices of assonance at verse terminals and by fashioning simple but brilliant jewels; he need not worry about rhyme, and he should hope to be a little vague and let the reader guess as to what lies beneath the literal meaning.

## SYMBOLISM, INDIRECTION, AND *KAONA*

The Hawaiian name for hidden meaning is *kaona*. The penchant for *kaona* or indirection is only partially explicable by the vagueness of the language occasioned in some parts by lack of sexual gender, verbs without subjects or objects, and verbless sentences, as indicated earlier. It may also be tied to the culture and to the value of pleasant interpersonal relationships, with an attendant failure to call a spade a spade, an adze an adze; and it may be linked with intellectual sprightliness and humor.

How prevalent is the *kaona* in Hawaiian songs? An extreme view was taken by Padraic Colum, the Irish poet who was hired by the Territorial Legislature in the early 1920's to compile a book of Hawaiian legends. He rewrote them in an Irish vein. He did not know the language, but saw hidden meanings everywhere, and he claimed (1924:337) that every Hawaiian poem had at least four meanings—an ostensible meaning, a vulgar meaning, a mythico-historical-topographical meaning, and a deeply hidden meaning. This hypothesis was sensibly answered by Mrs. Pukui (1949:247-251): "There are but two meanings: the literal and the *kaona*, or inner meaning. The literal is like the body, and the inner meaning is like the spirit of the poem. . . . There are some poems that have no inner meaning, and to read such meanings into them is folly."

To say that every poem has a vulgar meaning sounds like a comment by some of the more extreme nineteenth-century missionaries.

One perusing even a few songs is impressed by the constant references to ferns, *lehuas,* pandanus, fragrance, winds, rains, and wetness. The ferns, flowers, and birds in love songs refer to sweethearts; the theory will be offered shortly that water and rain and soakings also refer to sweethearts. The more obvious meanings of water and rain are life, fertility, growth, grief, and hardships.

Hawaiians love the rain and know that the beauty of their islands is due to rain. This is expressed succinctly in the saying on the water fountain in front of the Board of Water Supply Building in Honolulu: *Uwē ka lani, ola ka honua* (the sky weeps, the land lives).

Grief may be expressed, too, by rain, but postmissionary songs do not portray grief. The great rains of Hanalei in the song "Hanohano Hanalei" represent the beauty of this valley, with romantic overtones, but do not indicate grief as they do in the saying *Lu'ulu'u*

*Hanalei i ka ua nui, kaumaha i ka noe o Alaka'i* (Hanalei is downcast with great rains, heavy with the mists of Alaka'i).

In the chants, the rain, storms, and cold may be linked with hardship and trouble, as in the chant by a hula dancer who wants to be admitted to the hula school:

| | |
|---|---|
| *Eia ka pu'u nui o waho nei la,* | Great trouble outside here, |
| *He ua, he 'ino, he anu, he ko'eko'e.* | Rain, storm, cold, chill. |
| *E ku'u aloha e,* | My beloved, |
| *Maloko aku au* (Emerson, 1965:39) | Let me in. |

The only song in the present collection with such connotations is "Hole Wai-mea."

Hardship, like grief, is not discussed in the songs, which in general are happy and romantic, and the conclusion seems inescapable that—like the flowers—the rains, dews, waterfalls, wetness, soakings, winds, and coolness are romantically inspired. (This theory had been described by Elbert [1962] in a rather inaccessible publication.)

Even a glance at the songs in this collection will show that water, rain, sea spray, mist, coolness, and peace are nearly everywhere displayed. Here are some examples.

"Wet in fine and gentle rain,
Adornment of forest upland,
Bearer of sweetness
Coolness and palpitations."
      "Ka-'ili-lau-o-ke-koa"

"Drenched by the dew
She and I are two,
Three with the rustle of sea spray."
      "Hanohano Hanalei"

"Wet in the creeping rain,
You and I are there
In the fragrant forest."
      "Pulupē nei 'Ili i ke Anu"

"Finally I have known
Twofold peace;
We two in peace
Liquid spattering on the cliff."
      "Koni Au i ka Wai"

"We two in the spray,
Oh joy two together
Embracing tightly in the coolness,
Breathing deep of *palai* fern . . .
Oh such spray."
                    "Kāua i ka Huahua'i"


## THE POWER OF THE WORD

The early Hawaiians spoke no language other than their own, and may not have known of the existence of other languages. When they heard English they called it *namu* (gibberish). So, like the Stoic Greeks, they thought their names were universals with inherent nonarbitrary meanings. The meanings had power and explained the universe. In the section "Structure of the Hawaiian Language" we saw that the wrasse fish, *'a'awa,* was believed genetically related to *Piper mythisticum, 'awa,* because of a resemblance in the sounds in their names. The word had power: *I ka 'ōlelo nō ke ola, i ka 'ōlelo nō ka make* (in the word is life, in the word is death).

This was especially true in the religious chants, and efforts were made to preserve them unchanged throughout the centuries. A mistaken syllable might change the word and the new word might have connotations distasteful to a god, who might then cause the chanter's death. Many of the chants were sacred to the gods, including the family gods, and to the family. For this reason they were not freely imparted to passing strangers. They, as priceless heirlooms, were passed down to rightful heirs. The songs, such as those in this collection, are no longer sacred, nor are they family heirlooms. But still the sense that they were not to be freely bestowed has persisted in the face of mass acculturation and commercialism. This may be a reason for the rarity of song collections. Just as one's family stories and chants were not to be shared in publication, so were not the songs. We, the compilers of this collection, believe that we are not betraying secrets or friendships. We hope not. We believe that these songs—unlike so many chants—are no longer sacred, and that there is no longer the need to *'au'a* (hold back). And we hope that more people will be encouraged to sing Hawaiian songs more accurately and with greater understanding.

The word, however, is still powerful, and the composer even today must consider double meanings. Many composers avoid such words as *uli* (dark, foreboding) and *hala* (pandanus, pass away), but not all composers have these restrictions or we would not have so many songs about pandanus.

19

# TRANSLATIONS

Sapir has suggested (1939:237) that there may be two types of literary art: "a generalized non-linguistic art, which can be transferred without loss into an alien linguistic medium, and a specifically linguistic art that is not transferable." A Shakespearean play draws its sustenance from the intuitive record of experience, and is hence translatable, whereas a lyric by Swinburne "is as good as untranslatable."

Hawaiian legends (but not the chants that are in most of them) might belong to the first level of art, and the poetry, definitely to the latter. Nevertheless, an attempt at translation, but not at adaptation (which may surpass an original), is made in this collection. Our goal has been to produce an echo that will enable the singer who does not know Hawaiian very well to deduce the meanings of every content word in the song. Usually the Hawaiian content words are translated by single English content words; this sparseness, further, enhances the terseness of the Hawaiian. We believe that the singer will sing more intelligently if he knows of what he sings.

An effort also has been made to use a contemporary idiom and to translate the figures of speech rather literally. In some ways this makes the English better than the Hawaiian; a cliché in Hawaiian, such as rain creeping on a cliff, a streaked sea, an arching rainbow, or a flower that has been plucked, may sound fresh or virile in English. This type of "improvement" seems justified.


## POETIC VOCABULARY

A few of the poetic words, proper names, and phrases found frequently in the songs are listed. A few names with unfavorable connotations are also given. For details concerning the meanings of these words, see Pukui-Elbert, 1965.


### Birds *(manu)*

*ʻiʻiwi*  (scarlet honeycreeper)
*kaʻupu* (albatross)
*mamo*  (black honeycreeper)
*nēnē*  (Hawaiian goose)
*ʻōʻō*  (honey eater)
*pikake* (peacock)

## Chiefs    (*ali'i*)

| | |
|---|---|
| *Hanakahi,* | Hilo |
| *Kakuhihewa,* | Oahu |
| *Keawe,* | Hawaii |
| *Mano (Mano-ka-lani-pō),* | Kauai |
| *Pi'i-lani,* | Maui, especially of the bays beginning Hono- (Honokahua, Honokeano, Honokō-hau, Honokōwai, Honolua, Hononana) |

## Coolness

| | |
|---|---|
| *anu* | (cold) |
| *hu'ihu'i* | (chilly) |
| *ko'eko'e* | (damp cold) |
| *līhau* | (cool, wet, fresh) |
| *'olu'olu* | (cool, pleasant) |

## Fragrance

| | |
|---|---|
| *'a'ala,* | general term for fragrance |
| *kupaoa,* | strong |
| *moani,* | wafted |
| *onaona,* | soft |

## Fish and sea creatures    (*i'a*)

| | |
|---|---|
| *akule* | (goggle-eyed scad) |
| *ina* | (sea urchin) |
| *ka'ukama kai* | (sea cucumber) |
| *kole* | (surgeonfish) |
| *mā'i'i'i* | (Acanthrus) |
| *māikoiko* | (young surgeonfish) |
| *moi* | (threadfish) |
| *nenue* | (pilot fish) |
| *'ō'io* | (bonefish) |
| *'ōpelu* | (mackerel scad fish) |
| *ulua* | (crevally, sweetheart) |

(The bad-smelling *palani* fish is rarely mentioned. *Kūmū*, the beautiful red fish that is a recent slang for "sweetheart," does not occur in this collection.)

21

## Height

*heke*     (top)
*Himela*     (Himalayas)
*'io*     (hawk)
*'iu, 'iu'iu*     (paradise-like height)
*ki'eki'e*     (lofty)
*lani*     (royal chief, majesty, highness, prince, princess, king, queen)
*luna*     (high, top)
*piko*     (summit)
*wēkiu*     (summit)
*wēlau*     (summit)

## Mist

*noe,*     a general name
*'ohu,*     on a mountain
*uhiwai,*     heavy

## Flowers, plants, trees

*'a'ali'i,*     a tree
*'awapuhi*     (ginger)
*hala*     (pandanus)
*'ilima*     (flower of Oahu)
*kauna'oa*     (dodder, flower of Lanai)
*kāwelu,*     a grass
*kiele*     (gardenia)
*koai'e,*     a tree
*kukui*     (candlenut, the State tree)
*kupukupu,*     a fern
*lehua*     (flower of the *'ōhi'a* tree, flower of the island of Hawaii)
*laua'e,*     a fern
*lilia*     (lily)
*lokelani*     (rose)
*mamo*     (saffron flower)
*mokihana,*     a native tree, its leaves used for the flower lei of Kauai
*nēnē*     a grass
*'ohawai*     (lobelia)
*palai*     (fern)
*pīkake*     (jasmine)
*pili,*     a grass used for thatch

| | |
|---|---|
| *pua kalaunu* | (crown flower) |
| *pū'ili lau li'i* | (small-leafed bamboo) |
| *tuberose* | (tuberose) |
| *vibena* | (verbena) |

(The banana, an omen of misfortune and defeat, is not mentioned in love songs.)

## Love-making

| | |
|---|---|
| *'ano'i o ka pu'uwai* | (heart's desire) |
| *ho'oheno* | (infatuation) |
| *ho'onanea* | (relax) |
| *ho'oipo, ho'olipo* | (make love) |
| *'i'ini o loko* | (desire within) |
| *kili'opu* | (find delight) |
| *konikoni i ka pu'uwai* | (throbbing heart) |
| *la'i ke kaunu* | (passion calmed) |

## Mountains   *(mauna, kuahiwi)*

| | |
|---|---|
| Hale-a-ka-lā, | Maui |
| Ka'ala, | Oahu |
| Wai-'ale'ale, | Kauai |

## Rains   *(ua)*

| | |
|---|---|
| 'Āpa'apa'a, | Kohala, Hawaii |
| *hāli'i i ka nāhele* | (spread into the forest) |
| *'ino* | (storm) |
| Kani-lehua | (lehua-rustling), Hilo |
| Kīpu'upu'u | (goose-pimple raising), Wai-mea, Hawaii |
| *li'ili'i kilikilihune* | (fine and gentle rain) |
| *nihi pali* | (creeping along a cliff) |
| Pa'ū-pili | (moistening pili grass), Lahaina, Maui |
| Wa'ahila, | Manoa and Nu'u-anu, Honolulu |

## Sea   *(kai, moana)*

| | |
|---|---|
| *'ale* | (billows) |
| *hāwanawana* | (whispering), Ka-wai-hae, Hawaii |
| *malino* | (calm), Kona, Hawaii |
| *mā'oki'oki* | (streaked), Kona, Hawaii |
| *nalu* | (wave) |
| *nehe i ka 'ili'ili* | (rustling the pebbles) |

## Wetness

| | |
|---|---|
| *hau* | (dew) |
| *ho'opē* | (soaked) |
| *huahua'i* | (spray) |
| *kēhau* | (dew) |
| *pipi'i* | (bubbling) |
| *puia* | (drenched) |
| *pulupē* | (drenched) |
| *wai hu'ihu'i* | (cool water) |
| *wai kāpīpī* | (sprinkling water) |
| *wai konikoni* | (tingling water) |
| *wai noenoe* | (misty water) |

## Winds   *(makani, ahe)*

| | |
|---|---|
| A'e, | northeast tradewind |
| Kiu, | northwesterly wind |
| Kuehu lepo | (earth scattering), Ka'ū |
| Mālua | a sea breeze |
| Moa'e, | northeast tradewind |
| Pu'ulena, | a cold wind at Kī-lau-ea |
| *ulumano* | (buffeting) |

(The Kona wind, which is believed to bring sickness, is never mentioned in songs.)

## Some common phrases

*'auhea 'oe, 'auhea wale 'oe*
(listen, heed, where are you?)

*e ō*
(answer)

*ha'ina 'ia mai (ana) ka puana*
(tell the refrain or theme)

*he lei nō ku'u kino*
(a lei for my body)

*holunape a ka lau o ka niu*
(swaying of the leaves of coconuts)

*lei i ka noe*
(wearing mist as a lei)

*mea 'ole ke anu*
(cold is nothing, cold is no worry)

24

*mehe ala e 'ī mai ana*
(as though saying)

*nā kau a kau*
(season to season)

*pali lele koa'e*
(cliff where tropic birds fly)

*pili kāua*
(we will be together)

*pi'o ke ānuenue*
(arch of the rainbow)

*pua a'u i kui a lawa*
(flower that I string as a lei and bind)

*pua i 'ako 'ia*
(flower that has been plucked)

*pua mae 'ole*
(flower that never fades)

*wehi nō ka uka*
(adornment of the uplands)


## FOLK SONGS?

Can the songs be called folk songs? In the usual interpretation of the term they cannot, as folk songs are old and anonymous. None of these songs are really old. They are all post-European, and probably few predate 1850 or 1860. The composers of many of them are known, and songs are still being written by living composers.

If the songs cannot be called true folk songs, we may say that they have certain attributes of folk songs, namely subject matter and style, both of which have been discussed. We know that these are "authentic" from a comparison with prehistoric chants preserved by today's chanters and in volumes by Emerson (1909, 1915), Fornander (1916-1919), and Roberts (1926).

Another similarity to genuine folk music is that in general the songs are transmitted orally rather than by notation, and are sung from memory. This accounts in part for the difficulty of making a collection such as this, plus the understandable reluctance of many singers to part with things that today are precious to them, and only yesterday were protected by taboos.

This respectful attitude of many Hawaiians toward the songs is similar to folk attitudes in other cultures. The songs should not be tampered with, such persons believe, nor mixed or strung together in medleys. Traditional songs should not be jazzed up or crooned or made into rock-and-roll. Saxophones and steel guitars are frowned on by those with this attitude. They do not believe that the songs should follow the fleeting fads of the Top Ten. They should not *all* be sung fast, nor should they *all* be sung slow and dragging. They should be pronounced properly and they should not be used as experiments.

With this, paradoxically enough, is a certain freedom of mood and interpretation such as is probably not found with popular songs in the Western sense. This is very Polynesian and is akin to Polynesian resistance to routine and mechanization. One need not always sing the song in exactly the same way. Polynesian art more than much art elsewhere depends on display of personal charms and personality. Mechanical perfection or slavish imitation is never enough. The personality of the artist may and should shine forth in every song and dance.

# TRADITIONAL SONGS

## ADIOS KE ALOHA          ADIOS, MY LOVE

This song was composed by Prince Lele-iō-Hoku. Mexican cowboys at Wai-mea, Hawaii, added Spanish words (see "Hālona").

E kuʻu belle o ka pō laʻilaʻi,
Ka lawe mālie a ka mahina
Kōaniani mai nei e ke ahe
ʻAhea ʻoe hoʻolono mai.

O my belle of the peaceful night,
Feel the calm moon
Breeze-cooled
Calling you to listen.

*Hui*

ʻAhea (ʻoe), ʻahea (ʻoe),
ʻOe hoʻolono mai
I nei leo nahenahe.
Adios, adios ke aloha.

*Chorus*

Calling you, calling you,
Listen
To this soft voice.
Adios, adios my love.

E ka hauʻoli ʻiniki puʻuwai,
E ke aloha e maliu mai ʻoe,
Ke hoʻolale mai nei e ke Kiu,
Ua anu ka wao i ka ua.

O joy tingling heart,
O love, turn here,
The Kiu wind implores,
The depths are cool with rain.

Hoʻokahi kiss dew drops he maʻū ia,
E ka belle o ka noe līhau,
Eia au la e ke aloha,
Ke huli hoʻi nei me ka neo.

A single moist dew drop kiss,
O belle of the cool mist,
Here am I, O love,
Coming back with nothing.


## AHI WELA          HOT FIRE

The composer of the first of the two versions of this well-known song is not known. The composers of the second version (dated 1891) were Lizzie Doirin and Mary Beckley. Little girls sometimes sing and dance this hula. The words suggest that this is hardly an appropriate number for them.

### Older Version

Kuʻu pua i liʻa ai
Aʻu i kui a lawa
I lei hoʻohiehie
Nō ke ano ahiahi.

My flower desired
For me to braid and bind
An elegant lei
For evening time.

*Hui*

Ahi wela mai nei loko
I ka hana a ke aloha
E lalawe nei kuʻu kino
Konikoni lua i ka pō nei.

*Chorus*

Hot fire here within
The act of love
Overpowers my body
Throbbing last night.

28

'Elua nō māua
A i 'ike ia hana
La'i ai ka nanea 'ana
Ho'oipo i ku'u kino.

Two of us
Have felt the power
Peaceful relaxing
Making love within my body.

## Later Version

'Elua nō māua
I 'ike ia hana,
La'i wale ke kaunu
Ho'onipo i ka poli.

Two of us
Have felt the power,
Calm after passion
Making love within the heart.

*Hui*

Ahi wela mai nei loko
I ka hana a ke aloha
E lalawe nei ku'u kino
Konikoni lua i ka pu'uwai.

*Chorus*

Hot fire is here within
The act of love
Overpowers my body
And my throbbing heart.

'Auhea wale ana 'oe,
Ku'u pua i kui a lei,
I lei ho'ohiehie
Nō ke anu ahiahi.

Heed,
O flower of mine strewn in a lei,
An elegant lei
In the coolness of the evening.

## 'AHULILI

This song has numerous versions. The one following was given to Mary Kawena Pukui and Eleanor Williamson at Kau-pō, Maui, by Mrs. Francis Marciel (née Violet Poepoe) on December 1, 1961. 'Ahulili is a prominent peak easily seen from the lanai of Mrs. Josephine Marciel's home at Kau-pō. The song was composed many years ago by Scott Ha'i, a Kau-pō resident. Note the pun on Mt. 'Ahulili and *lili* (jealous). An alternate last stanza is *Ha'ina mai ka puana* followed by the first three lines of the first stanza.

He aloha nō 'o 'Ahulili,
A he lili paha kō iala
I ke kau mau 'ole 'ia
E ka 'ohu kau kuahiwi.

Love for 'Ahulili,
Perhaps she's jealous
Because not always rests
Mist upon the mountain.

Eia iho nō e ka 'olu,
Ke 'ala kūpaoa
Lawa pono kou makemake
E manene ai kou kino.

Here sweetness,
Heady fragrance
Enough for your desires
And your tingling body.

29

'Ako aku au i ka pua
Kui nō wau a lei,
A i lei poina 'ole
Nō nā kau a kau.

I have plucked the flower
Strung into a lei,
A lei never forgotten
From one season to the next.

Pa'a 'ia iho a pa'a
Ka 'i'ini me ka 'ano'i,
He 'ano'i nō ka 'ōpua,
Ka beauty o Mauna-hape.

Hold, hold fast to
Desire and yearning,
Yearning for the cloud banks,
The beauty of Mount-Happy.

E ō 'ia e ka lei,
Ke 'ala kūpaoa,
Ka puana ho'i a ka moe,
Ka beauty o Mauna-hape.

Respond, lei,
Heady fragrance,
The answer to dreams,
The beauty of Mount-Happy.

## 'ĀINA-HAU

'Āina-Hau (*hau*-tree land) was an estate near the site of the present Ka-'iu-lani Hotel in Waikiki that had belonged to Princess Ruth Ke'eli-kō-lani, but which she gave to her godchild, Ka-'iu-lani, at her baptism in 1875. The estate was planned and supervised by Ka-'iu-lani's father, Archibald S. Cleghorn (Kuykendall, 1967:112). The song was composed by Ka-'iu-lani's mother, Princess Likelike (sister of Ka-lā-kaua and Lili'u-o-ka-lani). R. L. Stevenson was a frequent visitor at 'Āina-Hau when Ka-'iu-lani was 13 years old. Cleghorn inherited the property at Ka-'iu-lani's death in 1899, and upon his death in 1910 he left it to the Territory for a park. The Territorial legislature did not accept the gift.

Nā ka wai lukini, wai anuhea o
  ka rose
E ho'opē nei i ka liko o nā pua.
Nā ka manu pīkake manu hulu
  melemele
Nā kāhiko ia o ku'u home.

Sweet water, cool water of the
  rose
Drenching flower buds.
Peacocks and birds with yellow
  feathers
Adorn my home.

Nā ka makani aheahe i pā mai
  makai
I lawe mai i ke onaona
  līpoa,
E ho'oipo ho'onipo me ke 'ala
  ku'u home,
Ku'u home, ku'u home i ka
  'iu'iu.

Wind blowing gently from the
  sea
Brings the fragrance of *līpoa*
  seaweed,
Love and delight and perfume
  for my home,
My home, my home
  paradise.

*Hui*

Nani wale kuʻu home ʻĀina-Hau
 i ka ʻiu,
I ka holunape a ka lau o ka niu,
I ka uluwehiwehi i ke ʻala o nā
 pua,
Kuʻu home, kuʻu home i ka
 ʻiuʻiu.

*Chorus*

So beautiful is my home
 ʻĀina-Hau in a paradise,
Swaying leaves of coconuts,
Verdant beauty and fragrant
 flowers,
My home, my home
 paradise.

## A KONA HEMA ʻO KA LANI

## THE KING AT SOUTH KONA

The music for two versions of this chest-slapping *(paʻi umauma)* hula is given by Roberts (1926:185-187), who stated that the song comes from Maui and is "an old stock hula tune for it was encountered again and again in different guises." The song honors Ka-lā-kaua but at the same time praises the Kona and Kohala districts of Hawaii. Well-known places mentioned are Ka-ʻawa-loa, Ka-wai-hae, Māhu-kona, and Kohala, with their associated poetic epithets. *Lē ʻī mai ʻo Kohala i ka nuku* (Kohala is crowded at the mouth) is part of a chant and a saying in the foolish intelligence report of Pūpū-kea to the Maui leader Kama-lālā-walu, that all the Kohala people had gone to the mouth *(nuku)*, probably the harbor mouth, leaving the island unprotected (Elbert, 1959:185); Kama-lālā-walu then invaded the island and was disastrously defeated. Note in the song the linked terminals *ʻehu, ehuehu; i ke kai, i ke kai; Ka-wai-hae, hae ana; naulu, uluulu; ka moana, ka moana.*

A Kona Hema ʻo ka lani
Nānā iā Ka-ʻawa-loa
ʻIke i ka laʻi o ʻEhu.
Ehuehu ʻoe, e ka lani,

The king at South Kona
Beholds Ka-ʻawa-loa
And senses the peace of ʻEhu.
The power of your majesty,

Ka helena aʻo Hawaiʻi la
Mālamalama nā moku,
Ahuwale nā kualono,
ʻIke ʻia ka pae ʻōpua.

Face of Hawaii
Islands radiant,
Ridges erect,
Cloud banks seen.

E kukū ana i ke kai,
I ke kai hāwanawana,
ʻŌlelo o Ka-wai-hae.
Hae ana, e ka naulu.

Rising in the sea,
In the whispering sea,
Voice of Ka-wai-hae.
O showers, pour forth.

31

Ka makani hele uluulu,
Kū ka 'e'a i ka moana,
Ka moana o Māhu-kona,
Ka makani 'Āpa'apa'a.

Lē'ī mai 'o Kohala
I ka nuku nā
    huapala.
Ha'ina 'ia mai ka puana
Ka lani Ka-lā-kaua.

Wind that mounts to gales,
Spray seethes in the sea,
The sea of Māhu-kona,
And the wind 'Āpa'apa'a.

Kohala is crowded
To the very mouth with handsome
    ones.
Tell the story
Of his majesty, Ka-lā-kaua.

## ALEKOKI

This is an example of the story-telling qualities of the old songs. Songs were pronounced clearly, the hearers listened carefully to the story being told, and the more stanzas the better. The monotony of the tune was counterbalanced by the interest in the words.

The hula "Alekoki" is sometimes attributed to Ka-lā-kaua, with music by Lizzie Alohikea, but N. B. Emerson (1909:108-110) stated that the song was composed in about 1850 by Prince Luna-lilo and refers to his disappointment in not being able to marry Victoria Ka-mamalu, the sister of Lot Kamehameha and Liho-liho.

Alekoki is the name of Nu'u-anu Stream seaward of Kapena Falls. Ma'ema'e is the hill above the juncture of Nu'u-anu and Pauoa streets. Māmala is Honolulu harbor. The spray flurries refer to opposition to the marriage. The wind carrying news is perhaps scandal. The singer finally finds other flowers—but does he sound happy?

Today Hawaiian words as exotics embellish English songs; formerly English words as exotics embellished Hawaiian songs; *piliwi* (believe) in the first verse was substituted for an earlier *mana'o*.

'A'ole i piliwi 'ia
Kahi wai a'o Alekoki
Ua ho'okohu ka ua i uka
Noho maila i Nu'u-anu.

Anuanu makehewa au
Ke kali ana i laila
Kainō paha ua pa'a
Kou mana'o i 'ane'i.

Unbelievable
Waters of Alekoki
Like the rains of the uplands
In Nu'u-anu.

Cold forsaken me
Waiting there
Believing certain
Your thoughts were of me.

32

Iō i 'ane'i au
Ka pi'ina a'o Ma'ema'e
He 'ala onaona kou
Ka i hiki mai i 'ane'i.

Here I am
At Ma'ema'e Hill
Where your sweet fragrance
Has come to me.

Ua malu neia kino
Mamuli o kō leo,
Kau nui aku ka mana'o
Kahi wai a'o Kapena.

This body is captive
To your voice,
Thoughts linger
At the waters of Kapena.

Pani a pa'a 'ia mai
Nā mana wai a'o uka,
Maluna a'e nō au
Ma nā lumi li'ili'i.

Blocked
Upland streams,
And I am above
In little rooms.

Mawaho a'o Māmala
Hao mai nei ehuehu
Pulu au i ka hunakai
Kai he'ehe'e i ka 'ili.

Outside Māmala
Spray flurries
And I am wet with foam
And sea slippery to the skin.

Ho'okahi nō koa nui
Nāna e alo ia 'ino,
'Ino'ino mai nei luna
I ka hao a ka makani.

One brave man
Faces the storm,
The storms above
And the blustering wind.

He makani 'aha'ilono
Lohe ka luna i Pelekane.
A 'oia pō uli nui
Mea 'ole i ku'u mana'o.

A wind bringing news
That the king of England hears.
This deep black night
Cannot worry me.

E kilohi au i ka nani
Nā pua o Mauna-'ala.
Ha'ina mai ka puāna:
Kahi wai a'o Alekoki.

I behold beauty
And the flowers of Mauna-'ala.
Tell the refrain:
Waters of Alekoki.

## 'ĀLIKA                    THE *ARCTIC*

Kamakau (1961:144) mentions the ship *Arctic* landing at Kauai between 1787 and Vancouver's arrival in 1792. An editor's note on the same page gives the first four verses. The song was later printed in Smith (1955:vol. 67, no. 9, pp. 26, 29). This hula illustrates the Hawaiian fondness for place names (rather imaginery here) and veiled risqué meanings. It is sometimes credited to Charles Ka'apa.

Aia i 'Ālika
Ka ihu o ka moku.
Ua hao o pa'ihi,
Nā pe'a i ka makani.

There in the *Arctic*
The prow of the ship.
Set firmly,
Sails in the wind.

| | |
|---|---|
| Ke liolio nei | Taut |
| Ke kaulu likini, | Rigging lines, |
| 'Alu'alu 'ole iho, | Not slack, |
| Nā pe'a i ka makani. | Sails in the wind. |
| | |
| 'A'ole i kau pono, | Not fixed, |
| Ka newa i ka piko. | The needle in the north. |
| Ka'a 'ē ka huila | The wheel turns |
| E niniu i ka makani. | Spinning in the wind. |
| | |
| Ke kau a'e nei | Placed |
| Ka ihu o Macao | The prow of the *Macao* |
| Ke iho a'e nei | Down |
| E komo 'Asia. | To go to Asia. |
| | |
| Me ke Kai Melemele, | The Yellow Sea, |
| Ke kōwā o Pelina, | Bering Straits, |
| Nani wale ka 'ikena, | A lovely view, |
| Nā pua i Sarona. | Flowers of Sharon. |
| | |
| I noho ka ihu | The prow sets |
| I ka piko i Himela, | Towards the Himalaya summit, |
| Ka hale lau pama | A palm-leafed house |
| Ho'omaha i ke kula. | For rest on the plains. |
| | |
| Ha'ina 'ia mai | Tell |
| Ana ka puana: | The refrain: |
| | |
| Aia i 'Ālika | There in the *Arctic* |
| Ka ihu o ka moku. | The prow of the ship. |

**Alternate versions of the second and third stanzas.**

| | |
|---|---|
| Ua hele a pa'ihi | Set firmly |
| Nā pe'a i ke kia. | Sails to the mast. |
| Ke liolio nei | Taut |
| Nā kaula pōlena. | Furled rigging. |

## 'ĀLIKA SPOEHR HULA        ALEXANDER SPOEHR HULA

This hula, Ka'upena Wong's first composition, honored Dr. Spoehr, director of the Bishop Museum, in December 1961 when he accepted the chancellorship of the East-West Center at the University of Hawaii. The rainbow is a symbol of the university and also of chiefs. Ka-iwi-'ula is the name of the area around the Bishop Museum.

| | |
|---|---|
| Pi'o mai ke ānuenue | The rainbow arches |
| Nou, e ka haku maika'i. | For you, O fine leader. |

34

Ua pono nā hana nui āu,
Māhalo 'ia e nā kini.

Your great work is right,
Approved by the multitudes.

Ho'olono mai 'o Ka-iwi-'ula
I ka leo kono mai uka
   mai.

Ka-iwi-'ula listens
To the voice calling from the
   uplands.

Ho'i mai e alaka'i nui
Nō nā pua o ka honua nei.

Come and lead firmly
The children of this land.

Ha'ina 'ia mai ana ka puana:
Me ke aloha 'Ālika Spoehr he
   inoa.
Me ke aloha 'Ālika Spoehr he
   inoa.

Tell the refrain:
Greetings, for Alexander Spoehr
   a name song.
Greetings, for Alexander Spoehr
   a name song.

## ALOHA 'OE          FAREWELL TO YOU

This most famous of all Hawaiian songs was for decades sung for every departing and arriving steamer. A rather ambiguous statement in *Hawaii's Story by Hawaii's Queen* (Liliuokalani, 1898:290) suggests that the song was composed while the queen was imprisoned in 'Io-lani Palace, but on a copy of the song in her own handwriting in the State Archives, are the place and date: Maunawili, 1877. According to popular belief, and according to an account by Helen Caldwell (1915:79), "the inspiration for the words and music of this composition was furnished by the fond parting embrace of two lovers, whom the queen discovered when returning over the pali from a horseback party on the other side of the island." Hawaiians say, but this has not been seen in print, that one of the lovers was Likelike, Lili'u's sister, who later married A. S. Cleghorn.

Lili'u once heard "Aloha 'Oe" sung at the funeral of a missionary friend. She was shocked. "This is a love song," she said afterwards, but was told that the song would live forever as a song of farewell.

The *lehua 'āhihi* in the song are a kind of *'ōhi'a* that on the rugged pali slopes suggest Japanese bonsai trees.

In the queen's notebook, the next to the last line is *I laila hia'ai nā manu,* with the same meaning as given below.

Ha'aheo 'ē ka ua i nā pāli
Ke nihi a'ela i ka nahele
E uhai ana paha i ka liko
Pua 'āhihi lehua o
   uka.

Proudly the rain on the cliffs
Creeps into the forest
Seeking the buds
And miniature *lehua* flowers of
   the uplands.

| *Hui* | *Chorus* |
|---|---|
| Aloha 'oe, aloha 'oe, | Farewell to you, farewell to you, |
| E ke onaona noho i ka lipo. | O fragrance in the blue depths. |
| One fond embrace, a ho'i a'e au | One fond embrace and I leave |
| A hui hou aku. | To meet again. |
| | |
| 'O ka hali'a aloha ka i hiki mai | Sweet memories come |
| Ke hone a'e nei i ku'u manawa. | Sound softly in my heart. |
| 'O 'oe nō ka'u ipo aloha | You are my beloved sweetheart |
| A loko e hana nei. | Felt within. |
| | |
| Maopopo ku'u 'ike i ka nani | I understand the beauty |
| Nā pua rose o Mauna-wili. | Of rose blossoms at Mauna-wili. |
| I laila ho'ohie nā manu, | There the birds delight, |
| Miki'ala i ka nani o ia pua. | Alert the beauty of this flower. |

## 'AUHEA 'O KA LANI LA? — WHERE IS THE ROYAL CHIEF?

This pebble hula honors Alexander Luna-lilo (1835-1874). The English translation is by Ruth Lei-lani Tyau. In the first stanza she rhymes alternating lines; in the second and third stanzas she has "r" sounds in the last words of each line. The translator has inserted "we" twice in the third stanza and has translated two place names: *mū* (crowd) and *wai* (water) as each name is repeated in neighboring lines. Both places are in Puna, Hawaii. After surfing, one bathed in fresh water, as in the third stanza.

| | |
|---|---|
| 'Auhea 'o ka lani la? | The royal chief, where is he? |
| Aia i ka he'e nalu | There, surfing |
| He'e ana i ka lala la, | On the long wave sliding out to sea, |
| Ho'i ana i ka muku. | On the short wave returning. |
| | |
| A ka nalu o Hō'eu la | On the Hō'eu surf |
| E uho'i a'e kāua | We both return |
| A pae a'e a i Kai-mū la | And land at the Sea-of-crowds |
| Ho'omū nā kānaka. | Where the natives gather. |
| | |
| 'Au'au i ka wai la, | We bathe in the water, |
| A'o Wai-'ākōlea, | The water-of-ferns, |
| Lu'u aku a ea maila, | We plunge and surface, |
| Kānaenae o ka lani. | A eulogy for the royal one. |
| | |
| Ha'ina mai ka puana la: | Let the theme be said: |
| Nō Luna-lilo nō he inoa. | An honor chant for Luna-lilo. |

# BEAUTIFUL 'ILIMA

The information about this well-known song was supplied by Emma De Fries, the granddaughter of the song's composer, Princess Emma Alexandria Kano'a De Fries, who wrote it in honor of her firstborn son. His name, John Alexander Liholiho Ka-lani-noho-pono-o-Lunalilo, was given by the composer and Queen Emma, the child's godmother. The last part of the long name was translated by Miss De Fries as "the sovereign who sat before Lunalilo." The name was intended to distinguish the child from Alexander Liholiho (Kamehameha IV). The date of the composition is not known, but Kamehameha IV died in 1863 and his wife, Queen Emma, in 1885. The song was arranged by Henry Berger. An alternate title is "Liholiho."

The *'ilima* is the flower of Oahu, and the *lei 'ilima* is one of the most beautiful of all leis; about five hundred flowers are needed for a single lei.

The chorus exists only in English.

| | |
|---|---|
| Onaona wale ia pua, | This flower is softly fragrant, |
| I ka miki'ala mau 'ia. | And quickly secured. |
| Hele a nohenohea | Lovely |
| I ka nou a ke kēhau. | When pelted by the dew. |

*Chorus*
O Beautiful *ilima*,
Choice of my heart.
O sweet and charming flower
Soft and lovely to behold.

## BILI BOI                    BILLY BOY

The song "Billy Boy" was brought from England to the eastern seaboard of the United States after the Revolutionary War and since then has been collected at such scattered places as Dorset, Worcestershire, Ontario, Vermont, Pennsylvania, Virginia, and Iowa (Luther, 1940:48-49). The older compiler of this collection has happy memories of his grandmother (born in 1849) singing this song to him as a child in Iowa. In Hawaii the missionaries changed the song from a funny story about Billy, whose wife was talented but a young thing who couldn't leave her mammy, to a moralistic admonishment to study books and thereby become rich. "Bili Boi" was printed in *Na Mele Hoonanea* (n.d.:48-49).

| | |
|---|---|
| I hea la 'oe, Bili Boi, Bili Boi? | Where have you been, Billy Boy, Billy Boy? |

*37*

I hea la ʻoe, Bili Boi, Bili
    Boi?
I ka hale kula wau, i ka ʻimi
    naʻauao,
Paʻakikī naʻe a ʻane loaʻa
    ʻole.

Ua komo anei ʻoe, Bili Boi,
    Bili Boi?
Ua komo anei ʻoe, Bili Boi,
    Bili Boi?
ʻAe, ua komo leʻa wau, a hoʻāʻo
    naʻauao,
Paʻakikī naʻe a ʻane loaʻa
    ʻole.

He puke anei kāu, Bili Boi,
    Bili Boi?
He puke anei kāu, Bili Boi,
    Bili Boi?
ʻAe, he puke maikaʻi koʻu a e
    ʻake e ʻike nō,
Paʻakikī naʻe a ʻane loaʻa
    ʻole.

Ua ʻike anei ʻoe, Bili Boi,
    Bili Boi?
Ua ʻike anei ʻoe, Bili Boi,
    Bili Boi?
ʻAe, ua ʻike iki nonaʻe nui ka
    naʻaupō,
Paʻakikī naʻe a ʻane loaʻa
    ʻole.

Aloha nui ʻoe, Bili Boi, Bili
    Boi,
Aloha nui ʻoe, Bili Boi, Bili
    Boi,
A i hoʻoikaika mau i ka ʻimi
    naʻauao,
E loaʻa nō me kona waiwai nui.

Where have you been, Billy Boy,
    Billy Boy?
I've been to school trying to
    learn to be wise,
But it's hard and I almost cannot
    do it.

Did you go in, Billy Boy, Billy
    Boy?
Did you go in, Billy Boy, Billy
    Boy?
Yes I went in with a smile to
    learn to be wise,
But it's hard and I almost cannot
    do it.

Have you got a book, Billy Boy,
    Billy Boy?
Have you got a book, Billy Boy,
    Billy Boy?
Yes I've got a fine book and I
    want to know it,
But it's hard and I almost cannot
    do it.

Do you know it now, Billy Boy,
    Billy Boy?
Do you know it now, Billy Boy,
    Billy Boy?
Yes I know a little now but I'm
    still as slow can be,
But it's hard and I almost cannot
    do it.

Good for you, Billy Boy, Billy
    Boy
Good for you, Billy Boy, Billy
    Boy
Just keep doing all you can and
    you'll learn to be wise,
And you'll do it and be very rich.

## ʻEKOLU ʻIOLE MAKAPŌ

ʻEkolu ʻiole makapō.
ʻEkolu ʻiole makapō.

## THREE BLIND MICE

Three blind mice.
Three blind mice.

'Ike i ka holo o lākou.

See them run.

'Ike i ka holo o lākou.

See them run.

Holo aku mahope o ka wahine
mahi'ai,

Running after the farmer's
wife,

'Oki 'ia ka huelo me ka pahi
kalai,

Cut off the tail with the carving
knife,

'Ike 'oe (i) kekahi mea i like me
neia,

Have you ever seen anything like
this,

'Ekolu 'iole makapō.

Three blind mice.

### Alternate version of the last four verses:

Holo lākou i ka wahine mahi'ai,

They run after the farming wife,

'Oki ka huelo me ka pahoa
kalai,

Cut off the tails with the carving
knife,

Hiki iā 'oe ke nānā ai

Can you see

'Ekolu 'iole makapō.

Three blind mice.

## 'EKOLU MEA NUI   THREE IMPORTANT THINGS

Composed by Robert Nā-wāhine, the "Three Important Things" are from I Corinthians 13, which ends "And now abideth faith, hope, charity, these three; but the greatest of these is charity."

'Ekolu mea nui ma ka
honua,

Three important things in the
world,

'O ka mana'o'i'o, ka mana'olana,

Faith, hope,

A me ke aloha, ke aloha ka i 'oi
a'e,

And aloha, aloha is the
best,

Pōmaika'i nā mea apau,

And everything is blessed,

Pōmaika'i nā mea apau.

And everything is blessed.

E nā mākua, nā keiki,

O parents, children,

Nā mamo a Iuda me
'Epelaima,

Descendents of Judah and
Ephraim,

E pa'a ka mana'o i ka pono i 'oi
a'e,

Think always that righteousness
is best,

Pōmaika'i nā mea apau,

And everything is blessed,

Pōmaika'i nā mea apau.

And everything is blessed.

## E NIHI KA HELE   TREAD SOFTLY

This song is attributed to the Healani Glee Club at the time of Queen Ka-pi'o-lani's trip to California and to England in 1887 to attend the jubilee of Queen Victoria, who is referred to in the chorus as *ka lani* (the royal one). The song is also known as "Ka-pi'o-lani," since it honors her. *E nihi ka hele* is a saying. Emerson (1965:94) translates the advice *e nihi ka hele, mai ho'olawehala* as "walk softly, commit no offense." In the story of Pele and Hi'iaka (Emerson, 1915:31) Hi'iaka gives counsel about the dangerous trip through the forests of Pana'ewa: *E nihi ka hele i uka o Puna, mai 'ako i ka pua o lilo i ke ala o ka hewaweha* (Approach cautiously the forests of Puna, do not pluck flowers lest you be lost in the pathways of error). The song here is an expression of love for the queen, a hope for calm seas, and an admonition that she tread softly in cold California and remember her crown and her loved ones at home.

E ka moana nui, kai hohonu,
E lana mālie kou mau 'ale.
E ka makani nui ikaika,
E pā aheahe mālie 'oe.

Great ocean, deep sea,
May your billows calmly float.
O great and mighty wind,
Blow gently.

*Hui*

E nihi ka hele mai ho'opā,
Mai pūlale i ka 'ike a ka maka.
Ho'okahi nō makamaka 'o ke
     aloha.
A hea mai 'o ka lani a e
     kipa.

*Chorus*

Tread softly, do not touch,
Do not rush to see.
True friendship is based on
     love.
When the royal one calls, one
     visits.

'Ike iā Kaleponi he 'āina anu,
Ke hau ho'okuakea i ka
     'ili,
Lamalama i ka 'ili o ke kama,
Ka wahine i ka 'iu o luna.

Behold California cold land,
Snow that bleaches white the
     skin,
Glowing skin of princess,
Lady of lofty eminence.

E hele me ka poina 'ole
E huli 'ē ke alo i hope nei.
Eia kō lei kalaunu,
'O ka 'ōnohi o Hawai'i.

Go and do not forget
To come back here again.
Here is your royal crown,
Hawaii is the heart.

## HĀLONA

Composed by J. Elia, Hālona is about a gulch and mountain in the Lahaina area of Maui. The Pa'ū-pili rain is also at Lahaina. Spanish words such as *bonito* (pretty) were used in Hawaiian songs composed at the time that Mexican cowboys were in the islands (see also "Adios ke Aloha").

E aloha a'e ana nō wau
I ka ua Pa'ū-pili
Ka ninihi ko'iawe
I nā pali mauka o Hālona.

I love
Rain that wets the *pili* grass
And creeping showers
In the dewy uplands of Hālona.

40

He aloha ku'u lei kiele la,
Me 'oe ke aloha bonito,
A hiki aku wau i laila la
Konikoni i ku'u pu'uwai.

A gardenia lei is my love,
Aloha *bonito* to you,
To whom I go
With throbbing heart.

## HANOHANO HANALEI      THE GLORY OF HANALEI

Alfred Alohikea, a popular Kauai musician and politician, wrote this song in the 1920's in honor of Hanalei Valley. He drew on traditional materials, such as the *limu o Manu'akepa* (the bright green algae growing on the shore), the streams of Molokama that flow tumbling to form the main stream in this valley, and Māmalahoa, a mountain peak. Alohikea, known as Uno to his friends, was a big man with a beautiful voice that was appealing to everyone, but especially to women. An informant says that his piercing eyes bewitched the fair sex. His political speeches consisted mostly of songs. Chants about Hanalei are given in Emerson (1915:45; 1965:133, 155, 210) and Elbert (1959:95, 97).

A well-known expression of grief is *Lu'ulu'u Hanalei i ka ua nui* (Hanalei is burdened beneath great rain). Two places associated with rain are Hilo and Hanalei.

Hanohano Hanalei i ka ua
   nui,
E pakika kahi limu o Manu'akepa.
I laila ho'i au i 'ike iho ai
I ka hana hu'i konikoni i ka
   'ili.
Aloha kahi one o pua rose
I ka ho'opē 'ia e ka hunakai.
'Akahi ho'i au a 'ike i ka nani.
Hanohano Hanalei i ka ua
   nui.

The glory of Hanalei is its heavy
   rain,
Slippery seaweed of Manu'akepa.
There I felt
Tingling cool sensation of the
   skin.
Greetings, O sand and rose flowers
Drenched by sea spray.
Never have I seen such splendor.
The glory of Hanalei is its heavy
   rain.

Kilakila kahi wai nā Molokama
I ke kau 'ia mai ho'i e ka 'ohu.
He 'ohu ho'i 'oe nō ka 'āina
A Hanalei a'e ha'aheo nei.
Kilohi i ka nani Māmalahoa
I ka ho'opē 'ia e ke kēhau.
'Elua wale iho nō māua,
I kolu i ka hone a ka 'ehu kai.

Majestic streams of Molokama
Mist-covered.
You are the mist of the land
That Hanalei cherishes.
Behold the beauty of Māmalahoa
Drenched by the dew.
She and I are two,
Three with the rustle of sea spray.

41

## HAWAI‘I ALOHA                 BELOVED HAWAII

This is one of the many songs composed by the Reverend Lorenzo Lyons, known as Makua Laiana, who had a church for many years at Wai-mea, Hawaii. He died in 1886. A variant title for the song is "Ku‘u One Hānau." The song is so popular with Hawaiians that the melody is used in other songs.

E Hawai‘i, e ku‘u one hānau e,
Ku‘u home kulaīwi nei,
‘Oli nō au i nā pono
    lani e.
E Hawai‘i, aloha e.

O Hawaii, O sands of my birth,
My native home,
I rejoice in the blessings of
    heaven.
O Hawaii, aloha.

*Hui*

E hau‘oli nā ‘ōpio o Hawai‘i nei
‘Oli e! ‘Oli e!
Mai nā aheahe makani e pā mai
    nei
Mau ke aloha, nō Hawai‘i.

*Chorus*

Happy youth of Hawaii
Rejoice! Rejoice!
Gentle breezes
    blow
Love always for Hawaii.

E ha‘i mai kou mau kini lani e,
Kou mau kupa aloha, e Hawai‘i.
Nā mea ‘ōlino kamaha‘o nō luna
    mai.
E Hawai‘i, aloha e.

May your divine throngs speak,
Your loving people, O Hawaii.
The holy light from
    above.
O Hawaii, aloha.

Nā ke Akua e mālama mai iā‘oe,
Kou mau kualono aloha nei,
Kou mau kahawai ‘ōlinolino
    mau,
Kou mau māla pua nani e.

God protects you,
Your beloved ridges,
Your ever glistening
    streams,
Your beautiful flower gardens.

## HAWAIIAN ROUGH RIDERS

This song honors Ikua (Ikuwā) Purdy and Archie Ka‘aua, two cowboys from Wai-mea, Hawaii, who with Jack Low, represented Hawaii at a rodeo in Cheyenne, Wyoming, in 1908. When the Hawaiians arrived at Cheyenne they were looked upon as curiosities and sometimes taken for Negroes, and they had trouble finding horses to practice on. Jack Low could not compete because of asthma, but Purdy won first place and Ka‘aua third place. Ikua was proclaimed world champion and won a standing ovation from the crowd.

The term "Rough Riders" was famous as the name for Theodore Roosevelt's cavalry regiment in the Spanish-American War. The cold Kīpu‘upu‘u rain is associated with Wai-mea and was the name of a cowboy club at the Parker Ranch. Puʻu-o-ka-lani (hill of the royal chief) is a nearby place. The chorus is strange: aches and pains are often associated with love. *Huʻi* (ache) suggests *huʻihuʻi* (cool), and coolness is loved in Hawaii and is often linked with romance.

Kilakila nā rough riders
Me ka ua Kīpuʻupuʻu,
Me ka nani aʻo Puʻu-o-ka-lani,
Me ka hae o ka lanakila.

Magnificent rough riders
And Waimea's cold rain,
With its beauty of Puʻu-o-ka-lani,
And the flag of victory.

*Hui*

Huʻi e, huʻi ʻeha,
Huʻi konikoni i ka puʻuwai.
Huʻi e, huʻi ʻeha,
Huʻi konikoni i ka puʻuwai.

*Chorus*

Aches, aches and pains,
Aches throbbing in the heart.
Aches, aches and pains,
Aches throbbing in the heart.

ʻAkahi hoʻi au a ʻike maka
Nā rough riders helu ʻekahi
Inu ana i ka wai aniani
E maʻū i ka puʻu ke
    moni.

Never have I seen
Such champion rough riders
Drinking sparkling waters
To wet the throat when
    swallowed.

Hanohano wale nā cowboy,
He makuʻu noho i ka lio,
Hālena pono ʻoe i ke kaula ʻili
I ka lawe o ka pipi ʻāhiu.

Wonderful cowboys,
Pommel saddle on the horses,
Pulling taut the lasso,
Bringing in the wild cattle.

Kaulana Ikuwā me Kaʻaua,
Nā ʻeuʻeu kīpuka ʻili.
Eia mai nā paniolo pipi,
Me ka nani o kuʻu home.

Famous are Ikuwā and Kaʻaua,
Spirited lassoers.
Here come the cowboys,
The glory of my home.

## HAWAIʻI PONOʻĪ        HAWAII'S OWN

According to Emerson Smith, *"Hawaiʻi Ponoʻī"* originated as another version of "God Save the King" with Hawaiian verses by King Ka-lā-kaua but was transmitted into a great anthem through the artistry of Captain Henry Berger." It was first sung in Ka-wai-a-Haʻo Church on November 16, 1874. The music and an English translation were printed in Smith (1955:vol. 67, no. 4, pp. 14-15, 26) and in Emerson (1909:172).

Hawaiʻi ponoʻī,
Nānā i kou mōʻī,
Ka lani aliʻi,
Ke aliʻi.

Hawaii's own,
Look to your king,
The royal chief,
The chief.

| | |
|---|---|
| Makua lani e,<br>Kamehameha e,<br>Nā kāua e pale<br>Me ka ihe. | Royal father,<br>Kamehameha,<br>We shall defend<br>With spears. |
| Hawai'i pono'ī,<br>Nānā i nā ali'i,<br>Nā pua muli kou,<br>Nā pōki'i. | Hawaii's own,<br>Look to your chiefs,<br>The children after you,<br>The young. |
| Hawai'i pono'ī,<br>E ka lāhui e,<br>'O kāu hana nui<br>E ui e. | Hawaii's own,<br>O nation,<br>Your great duty<br>Strive. |

## HE INOA NŌ KA-'IU-LANI

## A NAME SONG FOR KA-'IU-LANI

This is one of six name songs written by Lili'u-o-ka-lani for her niece and heir apparent, Ka-'iu-lani. Rainbows were symbols of royalty. Kauai is praised in the song because some of Ka-'iu-lani's relatives came from there. In the last stanza, Mano is short for Mano-ka-lani-pō, a famous Kauai chief. Naue (see "Nā Hala o Naue") on Kauai is noted for pandanus, and Makana cliff in the Hanalei District, for its fragrant ferns. Another name song for Ka-'iu-lani was written by Prince Lele-iō-Hoku.

| | |
|---|---|
| Lamalama i luna ka 'ōnohi la,<br>Kāhiko ua kōkō'ula<br>   la,<br>Ka hō'ailona kapu o ke kama la,<br>He ēwe mai nā kūpuna. | Rainbow patch flashing high,<br>Rain adornment on earth-clinging<br>   rainbow,<br>Sacred symbol of the child,<br>Lineage from the ancestors. |

| *Hui* | *Chorus* |
|---|---|
| A-ha-hā, ua nani ka wahine la,<br>A-ha-hā, ka nohona i ka la'i,<br>A-ha-hā, ua hele a nohea la,<br>Pua ha'aheo o ke aupuni. | Oh, oh, the girl is pretty,<br>Oh, oh, dwelling in peacefulness,<br>Oh, oh, so lovely,<br>Cherished flower of the nation. |
| Ki'ina ka wehi o ke kama la<br>I ka mokupuni o Mano.<br>Ka hala o Naue i ke kai la,<br>Laua'e 'a'ala o Makana. | Fetch the adornment of the child<br>On the island of Mano.<br>The pandanus of Naue by the sea,<br>Fragrant fern of Makana. |

## HE INOA NŌ KĪNAʻU      A NAME SONG FOR KĪNAʻU

The honoree of this popular hula is not the famous regent Kīnaʻu (flaw), the daughter of Kamehameha I, but an infant son of Princess Ruth born about the mid-1800's. A similar song is called "Liliʻu" and honors Queen Liliʻu-o-ka-lani; it was composed by Anton Ka-ʻō-ʻō, a hula master who was called on suddenly to stage a performance for the queen at the palace. He thereupon substituted Liliʻu for Kīnaʻu, but didn't remember the original chant perfectly, so there are some differences and probably fewer verses.

| | |
|---|---|
| Kīnaʻu e, noho nani mai. | O Kīnaʻu, sit in pretty fashion. |
| Kō kino e, kiʻi milimili. | Your body, a doll to play with. |
| Kō maka e, noweo wale. | Your eyes, so bright. |
| Kō papālina, e kukū ana. | Your cheeks, standing. |
| Kō ihu e, e hanu onaona. | Your nose, shall breathe soft fragrance. |
| Kō waha e, e māpu ana. | Your mouth, wafting perfume. |
| Kō poʻohiwi, kau mai i luna. | Your shoulders, placed high. |
| Kō lima e, ani peʻahi. | Your hand, swings fan-like. |
| Kō poli e, nahenahe wale. | Your bosom, so soft. |
| Kō ʻōpū, pahu wai lana. | Your stomach, a keg of floating water. |
| Kō kuli e, nuku moi oe. | Your knee, just a *moi* fish beak. |
| Kō wāwae, kiʻi palanehe. | Your feet, dainty fetching. |
| Haʻina ʻia mai ana ka puana: | Tell the refrain: |
| Kīnaʻu e, noho nani mai. | O Kīnaʻu, sit in pretty fashion. |
| He inoa no Kīnaʻu. | A name song for Kīnaʻu. |

## HE KANIKAU NŌ LELE-IŌ-HOKU      A DIRGE FOR LELE-IŌ-HOKU

This dirge by Liliʻu-o-ka-lani for her younger brother, who died of rheumatic fever at the age of 22 in 1877, reveals her marvelous command of the language. Abrupt use of personal names was not polite in Hawaiian songs, and she refers to her dead brother as *Ka Lani* and *kuʻu Lani,* translated here "Prince" and "my Prince." The prince's full name was Lele-iō-Hoku-ka-lā-hoʻolewa, and is said to commemorate the funeral of Kamehameha III, who died in December 1854; a translation is "flight on the day of the full moon, the day of the funeral."

Liliʻu refers to King Ka-lā-kaua as Ka-uli-lua, a name used for him in honorary chants. She refers to Princess Likelike by one of her less known names, Ka-pili.

45

The composer does not use the motif so common in Hawaiian lamentations, that of shared tribulations. Quite the contrary, in the third stanza she speaks of "serene associations" with her younger brother. The torn heart in the first stanza also seems to be a foreign concept. When Ka-lā-kaua became king in 1874 he quickly named Lele-iō-Hoku as heir apparent, hence the king's question in the second stanza.

The American minister, Henry A. Peirce, at the time wrote of the prince (Kuykendall, 1967:196): "Of correct morals, well-educated and accomplished, the late prince promised to become, had he lived to ascend the throne, a wise and popular sovereign."

He aloha paumākō,  
Hoʻohākuʻi nākolo,  
Haehae i ka manawa  
Iā ʻOe, e Ka Lani.

Grief-stricken love,  
Blow echoing and reechoing,  
Tearing the heart  
For you, O Prince.

*Hui*  
Lihaliha wale e Ka Lani,  
Ka ʻikena aku  
I kāu hiʻolani,  
Lōliʻi kāu hoʻoilo.

*Chorus*  
Heartsick, O Prince,  
To behold  
Your sleep,  
Your peaceful winter.

Ke uwē aku nei  
Ka-uli-lua i ke anu.  
ʻAuhea kuʻu pokiʻi,  
Ka hoʻoilina aupuni?

Weeps  
Ka-uli-lua in the cold.  
Where is my younger brother,  
The nation's heir?

Ua hui mālānai  
Mamua e noho nei,  
Ke hopu hewa nei  
Kō kino wailua.

Serene association  
Reigned before,  
Snatched wrongly  
Your body's spirit.

Eia ʻo Ka-pili e  
Ke haʻalipo nei,  
Āna lipo walohia  
Iā ʻoe e kuʻu Lani.

Here is Ka-pili  
Bent dark,  
Her dark agony  
For you, my Prince.

Pau kou hea ʻana mai  
ʻAuhea ʻoe, Kuahine?  
Pehea e pau ai  
Keia ʻeha nui?

Gone your calling  
Where are you, Sister?  
How will end  
This great sorrow?

## HELE AU I KALEPONI      I'M GOING TO CALIFORNIA

This hula, composed by Bina Mossman, concerns a man bound for California who asks his fiancée what he should bring her. The clothes she wants suggest post-World War I styles.

| | |
|---|---|
| Hele au i Kaleponi | I'm going to California |
| Ho'i mai, male | When I come back, we'll be |
|   kāua. |   married. |
| He aha kou makemake? | What do you want? |
| Pane mai 'oia ala: | She answered: |
| Pāpale ipu kapakahi, | A hat with a crooked brim, |
| Kāma'a hila lauli'i, | High-heeled shoes, |
| Kīhei kūweluwelu, | A fringed shawl, |
| Palekoki hapa nihoniho, | A scalloped petticoat, |
| Ame ka lole mū'ekeke'i. | And a short skirt. |

## HE MELE LĀHUI HAWAI'I      SONG OF THE HAWAIIAN NATION

Lili'u-o-ka-lani was asked by Kamehameha V to compose a national anthem; she did this in a week's time, and as leader of the Ka-wai-a-Ha'o choir, she introduced the song in 1866. Lili'u wrote:

"The king was present for the purpose of criticising my new composition of both words and music, and was liberal in his commendations to me on my success. He admired not only the beauty of the music, but spoke enthusiastically of the appropriate words, so well adapted to the air and to the purpose for which they were written.

"This remained in use as our national anthem for some twenty years or more, when my brother composed the words of the Hawaii Ponoi. He was at the time the reigning king, and gave directions to the master of the band to set these to music. He, being a German, found some composition from his own country which he deemed appropriate; and this has been of late years our national air." (1898:31-32)

Lili'u translated the title of the song "Hawaiian National Anthem." Emerson Smith (1955:vol. 67, no. 3, pp. 18-19, 22) discussed the song and printed the music.

| | |
|---|---|
| Ka Makua mana loa, | Very powerful Father, |
| Maliu mai iā mākou. | Turn to us. |
| E hāliu aku nei | We look |
| Me ka na'au ha'aha'a. | With humble hearts. |
| E mau ka maluhia | Peace forever |

O nei pae ʻāina
Mai Hawaiʻi a Niʻihau
Malalo o Kāu malu

On these islands
From Hawaii to Niihau
With Your protection

E mau ke ea o ka
  ʻāina
Ma Kou pono mau
A mākou mana nui.
E ola, e ola ka Mōʻī mau.

May the life of the land be
  preserved
By Your constant goodness
Our great power.
Long live, long live the King.

E ka Haku mālama mai
I kō mākou nei Mōʻī.
E mau kona noho ʻana
Maluna o ka noho aliʻi.
Hāʻawi mai i ke aloha
Maloko o kona naʻau
A ma Kou ahonui
E ola, e ola ka Mōʻī.

O Lord protect
Our King.
Long be his reign
On the royal throne.
Give compassion
Within his heart
Through Your forbearance
Long live, long live the King.

Malalo o Kou aloha nui
Nā liʻi o ke Aupuni
Me nā makaʻāinana,
Ka lehulehu nō a pau,
Kiaʻi mai iā lākou
Me ke aloha ahonui.
E ola nō mākou
I Kou mana mau.

Beneath Your great love
Chiefs of the nation
And the people,
Everyone,
Guard them
With patient love.
May we live
By Your everlasting power.

## HE ʻONO                DELICIOUS

The composer, Bina Mossman, here praises fish and in her "Niu Haohao" praises liquor. The many glottal stops impart staccato force. Pretty girls enjoy being compared to sweet-eyed *kole* fish.

Keu a ka ʻono ma ke alopiko la,
Kahi momona piko ka nenue la,
Lihaliha wale ke momoni aku la,
ʻO ka ʻōʻio halalē ke kai la,
ʻO ka ʻōpelu e pepenu ana la.
He ʻono toumi tou hoʻi tau i
  tou puʻu te momoni atu.
He ʻono a he ʻono a he ʻono
  ʻiʻo nō (he ʻono nō) a he ʻono
  nō.

Oh how delicious is the belly,
Rich belly of the pilot fish,
Oily good to swallow,
Bone fish to slurp the gravy,
Scad fish to dunk with.
Delicious, my, my, to swallow in
  your throat.
Delicious delicious real
  delicious (just delicious) just
  delicious.

48

Mai pi'ikoi 'oe i ke akule la          Don't try for *akule*
A he i'a a ha'i i ka hohonu la,        Fish of others in the depths,
Ho'i iho 'oe i kahi 'anae la           Come back for mullets
Me ka manini pūlehu 'ia la             And broiled mullet
'O ke kole e ka i'a maka onaona la.    And sweet-eyed *kole* fish.

(The last two verses of the first stanza are repeated.)


## HI'ILAWE

Composed by Mrs. Kuakini, this song, formerly known as "Hali'a-lau-lani," is most effective with slack-key accompaniment. It concerns a girl from Puna who has a love affair at Hi'ilawe waterfall in Waipi'o, Hawai'i. The chattering birds may refer to gossips. The shifting from first to third person adds to the subtlety and hence in Hawaiian eyes to the charm of the song. The girl, who is not bashful, calls herself *uhiwai, hiwahiwa* (or *milimili*), *lei 'ā 'ī*, and *'ala i hali 'ia mai*. The version given below is a new one. Lines in an older version that differ follow in parentheses. See "Wai-pi'o," another song about Hi'ilawe.


Kūmaka ka 'ikena iā Hi'ilawe          All eyes are on Hi'ilawe
Ka papa lohi mai (ka papa lohi        In the sparkling lowlands of
   lua) a'o Maukele.                      Maukele.

Pakele mau au, i ka nui manu          I escape all the birds
Hauwala'au nei, puni                  Chattering everywhere in
   Wai-pi'o.                             Wai-pi'o.

'A'ole nō wau, e loa'a mai            I am not caught
A he uhiwai au, nō ke                 For I am the mist of the
   kuahiwi.                              mountains.

He hiwahiwa au (a he milimili         I am the darling (a toy) of the
   ho'i) nā ka makua                     parents
A he lei 'ā'ī, nā ke                  And a lei for the necks of
   kupuna.                               grandparents.

Nō Puna ke 'ala, i hali 'ia mai       The fragrance is wafted from
                                         Puna
Noho i ka wailele a'o Hi'ilawe.       And lives at Hi'ilawe waterfall.

Ha'ina 'ia mai ana ka puana:          Tell the refrain:
Kūmaka ka 'ikena, iā Hi'ilawe.        All eyes are on Hi'ilawe.
(Nō Puna ke 'ala i hali 'ia          (The fragrance is wafted from
   mai.)                                 Puna.)

# HILO HANAKAHI

This song names various places on the island of Hawaii and things for which they were noted: rain, pandanus, wind, and sea. The listing is more or less in clockwise direction. The annual *makahiki* processions went in this order. 'Umi-ā-Līloa was strongly advised by his priests to travel in this fashion, as he was a high chief (Elbert, 1959:148-149). Mary Kawena Pukui (oral communication) says that old people advised her when seeking knowledge of the past to travel with her right (strong) arm on the side of the mountains, where strength lies; if one journeys for relaxation or to assuage grief, he journeys with the sea on his left (weaker) side, so that it may wash away his sorrows and tribulations.

Hanakahi was a famous chief of Hilo and a symbol of peace (Emerson, 1909:60-61). Hilo-Hanakahi is a section of Hilo towards Ke-au-kaha.

| | |
|---|---|
| Hilo, Hanakahi, i ka ua Kani-lehua, | Hilo, Hanakahi, rain rustling *lehua.* |
| Puna, paia 'ala, i ka paia 'ala i ka hala. | Puna, fragrant bowers, bowers fragrant with *hala.* |
| Ka'ū, i ka makani, i ka makani kuehu lepo. | Ka'ū, the wind, the dirt scattering wind. |
| Kona, i ke kai, i ke kai mā'oki'oki. | Kona, the sea, the streaked sea. |
| Ka-wai-hae, i ke kai, i ke kai hāwanawana. | Ka-wai-hae, the sea, the whispering sea. |
| Wai-mea, i ka ua, i ka ua Kīpu'upu'u. | Wai-mea, the rain, the Kīpu'upu'u rain. |
| Kohala, i ka makani, i ka makani 'Āpa'apa'a. | Kohala, the wind, the Āpa'apa'a wind. |
| Hāmākua, i ka pali, i ka pali lele koa'e. | Hāmākua, the cliff, the tropic birds flying cliffs. |
| Ha'ina ka puana, i ka ua Kani-lehua. | Tell the refrain, rain rustling *lehua.* |

# HILO MARCH

This famous march was composed by Joseph K. Ae'a, a member of the Royal Hawaiian Band and a friend of Lili'u-o-ka-lani, when he was told that the Princess had requested the band to accompany her on an official visit to Hilo. The town of Hilo was endangered by "the massive eruption of lava from Mauna Loa on the island of Hawaii which began on November 5, 1880 and continued for nine months. The main flow was in the direction of the town of Hilo"

50

(Kuykendall, 1967:236). The Princess arrived in Hilo on August 4, 1881 and attended Christian services to pray for the town of Hilo. Plans were made for earth barricades and possible dynamiting of the flow. Nevertheless, a celebration was held and "Hilo March," with an arrangement by Henry Berger, was played in August, 1881. Ae'a's original title was "Ke 'Ala Tuberose," and the song does not mention the crisis threatening Hilo. Princess Ruth at this juncture is said to have journeyed to the flow and to propitiate Pele threw thirty red silk handkerchiefs and a bottle of brandy into it. An informant told Mary Kawena Pukui that as a child he accompanied Ruth and saw her make the offerings and say to Pele "When I go, you go." On August 9 the flow stopped.

Emerson Smith (1955:vol. 67, no. 5, pp. 14-15, 26) stated that the last stanza was added as a "coda" in 1902. The Pu'ulena is a cool wind at Kī-lau-ea.

| | |
|---|---|
| 'Auhea wale 'oe e ke 'ala tuberose, | Heed, O fragrance of tuberose, |
| He moani 'a'ala i ke ano ahiahi | Fragrance wafted at evening time |
| Ua like me ka lau vabine | Like verbena leaves |
| I ka hoene i ka poli pili pa'a. | Singing in the heart tightly clasped. |

| *Hui* | *Chorus* |
|---|---|
| 'Ike hou ana i ka nani a'o Hilo | Behold again the beauty of Hilo |
| I ka uluwehiwehi o ka lehua, | And beautiful *lehua* growth, |
| Lei ho'ohihi hi'i a ka malihini | Cherished lei worn by visitors |
| Mea 'ole i ke kono a ke aloha. | Not indifferent to the call of love. |

| | |
|---|---|
| E aloha a'e ana i ka makani Pu'ulena, | Greeting the Pu'ulena wind, |
| Ka makani kaulana o ka 'āina, | Famous wind of the land, |
| Home noho a nā 'i'iwi pōlena | Home of scarlet honey-creepers |
| Mea 'ole i ke kono a ke aloha. | Not indifferent to the call of love. |

| | |
|---|---|
| Nani wale nō Hilo | Hilo is so beautiful |
| I ka ua Kani-lehua | With the rain rustling *lehua* |
| Mehe mea ala e 'ī mai ana | As though saying |
| Eia iho a hiki mai. | Wait until the princess comes. |

Portions of this stirring song have been given by Emerson (1909:68-70), Roberts (1926:92-95, 234-235), and Fornander (vol. 6:202-203). Details vary considerably, which is not surprising in chants as old as this. Mrs. Pukui reports that the original chant is said to have been a name song for Kamehameha I that was inherited by his son, Liholiho. The Kīpuʻupuʻu were a band of runners who named themselves after Wai-mea's icy rain. Kamehameha is said to have asked that they be trained in spear fighting. They went to the forests called Mahiki and Wai-kā to strip (hole) the bark of saplings to be made into spears. (The title of the song is translated freely). Hilo here is a symbol of hardship, violence, and travail, as are the three winds mentioned in the songs. But even a Hawaiian war song has veiled references to love making. According to Winne (1968:201), the song based on the chant was composed by Prince Lele-iō-Hoku, presumably as leader of the famous Ka-wai-hau Glee Club. One source gives the date as 1889, long after the prince's death.

Hole Wai-mea i ka ihe a ka
  makani.
Hao mai nā ʻale a ke
  Kīpuʻupuʻu.
He lāʻau kalaʻihi ia na ke anu
I ʻōʻō i ka nahele o
  Mahiki.

Wai-mea strips the spears of the
  wind.
Waves are tossed in violence by
  the Kīpuʻupuʻu rains.
Trees brittle in the cold
Are made into spears in Mahiki
  forest.

*Hui*

Kū aku i ka pahu,
Kū a ka ʻawaʻawa,
Hananeʻe ke kīkala o kō Hilo
  kini
Hoʻi luʻuluʻu i ke one o
  Hanakahi.

*Chorus*

Hit by the thrusts,
Hit by the cold,
The hips of Hilo's throngs
  sag
As they return burdened to the
  sands of Hanakahi.

Kū akula i ka mala a ke
  Kīpuʻupuʻu
Holu ka maka o ka ʻōhāwai a
  Uli
Niniau ʻeha ka pua o ke
  koaiʻe,
Ua ʻeha i ka nahele o Wai-kā.

Pelted, and bruised by the
  Kīpuʻupuʻu rains
Lobelia petals of the sorceress
  sway
And *koaiʻe* flowers droop in
  pain,
Pangs in Wai-kā forest.

52

| | |
|---|---|
| Hoe Puna i ka wa'a, pālolo a ka 'ino, | Puna paddles canoes, mired in the storm, |
| Ho'oheno i nā hala o Ko'oko'olau, | Beloved pandanus of Ko'oko'olau, |
| Ua 'eha i ke ku'iku'i a ka Ulumano | Hurt by buffeting winds |
| Hala a'e ka makawalu ihe a ke A'e. | As the many spears of the A'e wind pass by. |

In one of Roberts' chanted renditions of the first and second stanzas, many k's are replaced by t's according to the following scheme, with t or k as noted in successive verses:

| Stanza 1 | Stanza 2 |
|---|---|
| t t t | k k k t t |
| t t | t k k |
| k t | k — k |
| t k | t k |

In Roberts' other version, the chanter used only two t's. This indicates the random substitution of one sound for the other—which to the chanter are one and the same sound. The only discernible pattern is that the chanter has used in the first stanza five successive t's, then some switching between t and k, whereas in the second stanza, k is the most commonly used.

| **HOLOHOLO KA'A** | **JOY RIDE** |
|---|---|

Words and music are by Clarence W. Kinney and were probably composed when speeding cars were somewhat of a novelty, roads were crooked, and breakdowns frequent. The "numbers" are those on the speedometer that fascinate the girl as they rotate.

| | |
|---|---|
| Kāua i ka holoholo ka'a, | You and I on a joy ride, |
| 'Oni ana ka huila lawe a lilo, | Wheels turn and carry far away, |
| Ku'u aku 'oe a pau pono | Just relax until no more |
| Nā huahelu e kau ana. | Numbers coming up. |
| | |
| 'Alawa iho 'oe ma ka 'ao'ao, | Glance to the sides, |
| Hū ana ka makani hele uluulu. | Wind whistles come in gusts. |
| Mea 'ole ka pi'ina me ka ihona | Climbing going down no matter |
| Me nā kīke'e alanui. | Or winding roads. |
| | |
| 'O ka pā kōnane a ka mahina, | The moon shines brightly, |
| Ahuwale nō i ka pae 'ōpua. | Fair upon the cloud towers. |
| Eia kāua i ka pi'ina pau | We are on the heights up there |
| A huli ho'i mai kāua. | But turn and go back. |

He manaʻo koʻu i ke kani
   koʻele,
Ua haki ka pilina aʻo luna iho.
He laʻi pono ke kaunu ʻana,
He nanea mai hoʻi kau.

Haʻina kō wehi e kuʻu lei.
Ke huli hoʻi nei kāua,
Honi aku ʻoe i ka ʻailea,
Ke ʻoni nei ka huila.

I worry about the clanking
   sound,
Springs broken top to bottom.
Passion calmed,
So delightful.

Sing your song my beloved.
We go home,
Breathing gasoline,
Wheels turning.

## HOʻOHENO            INFATUATION

This *hīmeni* is by two persons known to Queen Liliʻu-o-ka-lani. Jack Heleluhe wrote the words, and Joseph K. Aeʻa, the music. The English translation is by Ruth Lei-lani Tyau. Liʻa is a forest goddess frequently mentioned in songs, presumably because her name means "desire."

ʻAuhea ʻoe e ka ipo peʻe
   poli,
ʻO ke anoano wailiʻulā.
A he lei mamo ʻoe nō ke
   ahiahi
E ʻuhene ai me Liʻa i ka
   uka.

Listen, lover with a hidden
   heart,
Overpowering mirage.
You are evening's lei of
   saffron flowers
Exulting with Liʻa in the
   forest.

*Hui*            *Chorus*

Hoʻoheno mai ana ke aloha
   iaʻu
Mehe kui houhou ala i kuʻu
   poli,
He hāliʻa mau ia nō ka
   midnight,
Nō ka pō huʻihuʻi ke hau
   anu.

Hāmau ka ua la e ka
   hoa,
ʻOiai eia i ka nuku wai.
Waiwai paʻa ka manaʻo
   iā ʻoe
I ka nihi i ka welelau
   pali?

Love displays her
   affection
With a needle piercing my
   heart,
An enduring memory of the
   midnight,
The cold night and tingling
   dew.

The rain is silent, my
   companion,
Here at the stream's source.
Isn't the true source of
   wealth, the memory of you
On the brink—on the pali's
   tip?

Me 'oe ka 'ano'i pau 'ole,
A nei pu'uwai e 'oni nei.
Mai ho'ohala i ka 'ike lihi
   mai
Pulupē ai māua i ka ua
   noe.

With you an unending desire,
Here in the beating heart.
Do not thrust away the
   glimpse
Of our drenching in the
   misty rain.

## HULA O MAKEE

## THE *MAKEE* HULA

The *Makee* was a ship named for a rancher of the same name. The *Makee* went on the reef at Kapa'a, Kauai, and was found by the ship *Malulani*. Makee here represents a girl who has deserted her lover, Malulani, who is looking for her. Hiram was an officer of the ship. 'Ie'ie is the channel between Kauai and Oahu.

'Auhea iho nei la 'o Makee?
A ka Malulani la e huli hele nei.

Where is the *Makee?*
The *Malulani* looks everywhere.

Aia aku nei kahi i Kapa'a
Ka waiho kapakahi i ka 'āpapa.

There she is at Kapa'a
Keeled over on the reef.

'O ke kani honehone a ke oeoe
A e ha'i mai ana la i ka lono.

Softly sounds the whistle
Telling the news.

'O ka hola 'umi ia o ke aumoe
Kā'alo Malulani mawaho pono.

Ten o'clock at night
The *Malulani* passes by.

Kū mai Hailama pa'a i ka
   hoe
I mua a i hope ke kulana nei.

Hiram stands and grasps the
   paddle
Careening bow to stern.

Ākea ka moana nou e Makee,
Ma ke kai holuholu o ka 'Ie'ie.

Broad is your ocean, O *Makee,*
And the swaying seas of 'Ie'ie.

Ha'ina 'ia mai ana ka puana:
'Auhea iho nei la 'o Makee?

Tell the refrain:
Where is the *Makee?*

## IĀ 'OE E KA LĀ E 'ALOHI NEI

## FOR YOU, O GLITTERING SUN

Composed in 1881 by Queen Ka-pi'o-lani's cousin, Nā-hinu, of Kauai, in honor of Ka-lā-kaua before he left on his world tour. The Hawaiians were not sun worshippers, and this is perhaps the only reference in this collection to the sun. The Himalayas, so dazzlingly lofty, were popular along with other words for height as praise of royalty (see " 'Ālika," "Palisa"). The stamping on taboos recalls the exemption of royal chiefs in legends from the taboos of ordinary persons.

| | |
|---|---|
| Iā 'oe e ka lā e 'alohi nei | For you, O glittering sun |
| Ma nā welelau a'o ka honua. | On the summit of the world. |
| | |
| Hō'ike a'e 'oe a i kou nani | Show your glory |
| I ka malamalama 'oi kelakela. | At its greatest brilliance. |
| | |
| Nāu i noi'i nowelo aku | You seek and delve |
| Pau nā pali pa'a i ke 'ike 'ia. | All firm cliffs are seen. |
| | |
| 'Ike 'oe i ka nani a'o | You've seen the beauties of the |
| Himela | Himalayas |
| I ka hene wai'olu lawe mālie. | And its gentle slopes so calm. |
| | |
| He mauna i lōhia me ke | A mountain suffused with |
| onaona | fragrance |
| Kaulana i ka nani me ke | Famous for beauty and |
| ki'eki'e. | height. |
| | |
| Ki'eki'e 'o ka lani noho mai | His royal highness lives |
| i luna | above |
| Nāna i hehei ia kapu o | He stamps upon taboos of |
| Kahiki. | foreign lands. |
| | |
| Heihei kū ana i ka nuku 'ale | Racing on the tops of waves |
| I ke kai hāla'i lana mālie. | In calm sea floating serenely. |
| | |
| Ha'ina 'ia mai ana ka puana: | Tell the refrain: |
| E ola e ka lani a mau loa. | May you live long, O Majesty. |

| 'INIKI MĀLIE | GENTLE PINCHES |
|---|---|

This song concerns the winds of Maui.

| | |
|---|---|
| Wai-kapū, makani kokololio. | Wai-kapū, wind in gusts. |
| *Hui* | *Chorus* |
| Makani houhou 'ili | Skin-stinging wind |
| 'Inikiniki mālie | Gently pinching. |
| (*or* 'inisinisi mālie). | |
| Wai-luku, makani lawe māile. | Wai-luku, wind becoming gentle. |
| Wai-ehu, makani hō'eha 'ili. | Wai-ehu, wind paining skin. |
| Wai-he'e, makani kili'o'opu. | Wai-he'e, wind graceful. |
| Ha'ina 'ia mai ana ka puana. | Tell the refrain. |

56

## KA BANA KINAI RAMA          RUM-QUENCHING BAND

Temperance songs were published in Protestant newspapers in the mid-1800's. The tune of this one is not known to the compilers.

| | |
|---|---|
| Mai kali 'ē nō ka lā 'ē a'e. | Don't wait until another day. |
| Ka lā 'ānō ka lā maika'i | Today's a good day |
| E hui me ka Bana nei, | To join the Band, |
| Ka Bana kinai rama. | The rum-quenching Band. |
| E hui mai nā kamali'i, kamali'i, kamali'i! | Children children children, join! |
| E hui ku'ikahi mai, | Unite, |
| A kū'ē a mau i ka rama. | Fight rum forever. |
| | |
| Ua hune 'ē nā 'ohana nei, | The family's poor, |
| Ua nāhaehae ka lole e, | The clothing torn, |
| Pōloli nō nā kamali'i. | The children hungry. |
| A nō ke aha keia? | Why? |
| Ka hana a ka rama nei, rama nei, rama nei. | The work of rum, rum, rum. |
| E hui mai nā kamali'i, | Children, join, |
| A kū'ē a mau i ka rama. | Fight rum forever. |

| *Hui* | *Chorus* |
|---|---|
| Hui mai ma ka Bana nei | Join the Band |
| Ka Bana i kaulana e | Famous Band |
| Ka Bana koa inu wai | Band of water-drinking soldiers |
| Ka Bana kinai rama. | Rum-quenching Band. |

## KA-'ILI-LAU-O-KE-KOA

This *hīmeni* by Henry Waia'u is based on the Kauai legend of the same name (Rice, 1923:106-108). Ka-'ili-lau-o-ke-koa (the leaf surface of the *koa* tree) was a princess whose *kahu* (attendant) awakened her late one night to listen to a mysterious and beautiful wafted melody of a nose flute *(hano)*, an instrument that could relay actual speech, especially matters of the heart. Next night Ka-'ili again heard the flute and this time it called out her name and asked if she slept. She then journeyed in search of the flute through rain and mist far up the Wai-lua River to a fey place called Pihana-ka-lani (abode of supernatural beings), and here she found the flute in the bosom of a strange young man. She fell in love. Her parents protested bitterly at what seemed a misalliance. Later the musician proved to be a chief and we have a happy ending. In this song is a fine Hawaiian definition of rain and its functions. See a chant, perhaps about the same princess, in Emerson (1909:135–137).

| Hui | Chorus |
|---|---|
| Kani 'ē ka wī, | Tinkle, tinkle, |
| 'Uhē, 'uhe'uhene, 'uhe'uhene, | La, tra-la, tra-la, |
| E Ka-'ili-lau-o-ke-koa, | O Ka-'ili-lau-o-ke-koa, |
| 'auhea 'oe, | listen, |
| E Pihana-ka- | Pihana-ka-lani, gathering place |
| lani, | of kings, |
| E Ka-'ili-lau-o-ke-koa, | O Ka-'ili-lau-o-ke-koa, |
| Ua moe paha 'oe, 'a'ole la? | You are asleep, no? |
| | |
| Ma'ema'e wale ke kino o ka | So clean is the body of the |
| palai | fern |
| Pulupē i ka ua li'ili'i | Wet in fine and gentle |
| kilikilihune | rain |
| A he wehi ia nō ka uka o ka | Adornment of forest |
| nahele, | upland, |
| He moani ke 'ala i lawe 'ia mai, | And the bearer of sweetness, |
| Hu'ihu'i, konikoni e. | Coolness, and palpitations. |

## KA MAKANI KĀ'ILI ALOHA

## LOVE SNATCHED BY THE WIND

Composed by Matthew H. Kāne, this is a song of a Maui man who had been deserted by his wife. A *kahuna* gave him a potion which he threw into the sea at a place where his wife often fished. The wife later returned to him. A quilt pattern on Maui is called *ka makani kā'ili aloha.*

| | |
|---|---|
| E aloha a'e ana nō au | I love |
| I ka makani kaulana o ka | Famous wind of the |
| 'āina. | land. |
| A'u e ho'oheno nei | My beloved |
| Ka makani kā'ili aloha. | Snatched by the wind. |

| Hui | Chorus |
|---|---|
| Ku'u pua, ku'u lei, ku'u | My flower, my lei, my |
| milimili e, | toy, |
| Ku'u lei kau i ka wēkiu, | My lei placed supreme, |
| A he milimili 'oe, a he | You my toy, my |
| hiwahiwa na'u, | pride, |
| A he lei mau nō ku'u kino. | A lei forever for my body. |

58

I aloha ʻia nō ia home,
Ia home luakaha a ka
    malihini
Aʻu i noho ai a kupa
Ka makani kāʻili
    aloha.

This home beloved,
This home delightful to
    visitors
Where I have stayed long years
With the love once snatched by
    the wind.

## KĀMAU KĪʻAHA

One of the few toasting songs.

Kāmau kīʻaha i ʻolu,
E paheʻe i kō puʻu ke
    moni.
Mai kuhi mai ʻoe kā haʻi
I kō alawiki ʻana mai.

## TIP THE GLASS

Tip the glass for comfort,
Let it slip down your throat
    with a swallow.
Don't covet someone else's
In your haste.

## KA MOAʻE

Composed by Solomon Hiram. Māʻihi is a place in Kona.

ʻAuhea wale ʻoe e ka Moaʻe
E lawe hele nei i kuʻu
    aloha.

Ahea la ʻoe hoʻihoʻi mai
A he lei poina ʻole ia naʻu?

A he wehi kāhiko nō kuʻu
    kino,
A he hoa i ke anu pili hemo
    ʻole.

E lei aku ʻoe i kuʻu aloha
I koʻolua nou nō kahi
    mehameha.

Mai noho ʻoe a hoʻopoina
I kahi pōkē pua lalana.

A kāua la i kui iho ai
Kāhiko nō ka pō ua
    liʻiliʻi.

Ilihia hoʻi au i kō
    leo
I ka pane ʻana mai me ka
    nahenahe.

## THE TRADEWIND

Listen, O Tradewind
Who scatters my loves here and
    there.

When will you return
The lei I never will forget?

She is a fine adornment for my
    body,
A friend never to leave me
    when I am cold.

Wear my love as a lei
And as your companion in lonely
    places.

Do not forget
This warm bouquet of flowers.

We shall be interwoven
As blessings for nights with
    fine rain.

I will be thrilled by your
    voice
And your soft
    answers.

I he aha nei hana nui au
E haʻi mai ʻoe, e kuʻu aloha.

Whatever I am doing
Just call me, my love.

He aloha i pili ʻia e ke onaona,
Kuʻu ipo i ke kai malino aʻo
    Kona.

Love united in sweetness,
My sweetheart of the quiet seas
    of Kona.

Nō Kona mai nō ke kai malino
Nā hau o Māʻihi e kaulana nei.

From Kona's quiet seas
Famous dew of Māʻihi.

Haʻina ʻia mai ka puana:
Kuʻu ipo i ke kai malino aʻo
    Kona.

Tell the story:
My sweetheart of the quiet seas
    of Kona.

## KAMUELA KING        SAMUEL KING

This political song was composed by J. (Koana) N. Wilcox in honor of Samuel Wilder King when he was running for delegate to the U.S. Congress in 1936. Before statehood and television, nearly every candidate for important offices had his own singing and hula troupe.

Kaulana Kamuela King i kou
    inoa,
Ka ʻelele lāhui i
    Wakinekona.

Honored is Samuel King with
    your name song
The people's delegate in
    Washington.

He pua nani ʻoe nō Hawaiʻi
A ka lehulehu aʻe hiʻipoi nei.

You are a fine flower of Hawaii
Cherished by its throngs.

E ala e Hawaiʻi nui
    ākea,
Lōkahi ka manaʻo me ke
    aloha.

Arise! All of you from broad
    Hawaii,
Stand together in unity and
    love.

Ka Makua mau loa kou
    kōkua,
Ka Mana Kahikolu kou alakaʻi.

The everlasting Father your
    help,
The Holy Trinity your guide.

E ō e Kamuela King i kou
    inoa,
Ka ʻelele lāhui i
    Wakinekona.

Respond to your name song,
    Samuel King,
The people's delegate in
    Washington.

## KĀNE-ʻOHE

This hula was composed by Abbie Kong (soloist with the Royal Hawaiian Band in the late 1930's) and Johnny Noble to honor the installation of electricity at Kāne-ʻohe, Oahu. The symbolic connotations of rain, peace, and coolness mentioned in the chorus are discussed by Elbert (1962). The places mentioned in the song are in the vicinity of Kāne-'ohe. Noble was a well-known musician and composer in the 1920's and 1930's; he published a song book and composed many popular *hapa-haole* songs.

'Ōlapa ka uila i Kāne-'ohe
Ka hui laulima o 'i Lani-wai
   (*or* Hi'i-lani-wai).

Light flashes at the Kāne-'ohe
Cooperative society at
   Lani-wai.

*Hui*

*Chorus*

Me ka ua a Puakea,
Ka la'i a'o Malūlani (*or*
   Mololani),
Me ke anu o ke Ko'ōlau.

The Puakea rain,
The peace of
   Malūlani,
And the coolness of the Kō'olau.

Kaulana mai nei Ko'olau-poko
Ua 'ā ka uila a'i Kāne-'ohe.

Ko'olau-poko is famous
And lights go on at Kāne-'ohe.

Hanohano Mō-kapu i ka 'ehu
   kai,
Te tua motumotu a'o He'eia.

The glory of Mō-kapu is the sea
   spray,
And the jagged ridge of He'eia.

Ho'okahi meahou ma He'eia:
Ka uwea kelekalepa leo nahenahe.

The news at He'eia:
Sweet-voiced telegraph wire.

Aia 'ike lihi o ka 'āina
Kahi a ke aloha i walea ai.

Glimpses of the land
Where love finds delight.

Walea ana 'oe me ke onaona,
Ku'u lei hulu mamo pili i ke
   anu.

Delight with the sweet one,
With my *mamo* feather lei in the
   coolness.

Ua ana ho'i au a i kō leo,
Kō pane 'ana mai pehea au.

I am happy with your voice,
Your answer how am I.

Ha'ina 'ia mai ana ka puana:
Ua 'ā ka uila a'i Kāne-'ohe.

Tell the refrain:
Lights go on at Kāne-'ohe.

## KĀUA I KA HUAHUA'I     WE TWO IN THE SPRAY

Because of its lively tune, this song is presented to tourists as "the Hawaiian war chant." It is actually a love song. It was composed by Lele-iō-Hoku, brother of King Ka-lā-kaua and Queen Lili'u-o-ka-lani. Emerson (1909:165) suggests that this song dates from the 1860's or soon thereafter. The six glottal stops in the first three verses add to the nervous excitement of the song and perhaps make it sound warlike.

Many singers replace the k's with t's.

| | |
|---|---|
| Kāua i ka huahuaʻi, | We two in the spray, |
| E ʻuhene la i pili koʻolua | Oh joy two together |
| Pukukuʻi lua i ke koʻekoʻe, | Embracing tightly in the coolness, |
| Hanu lipo o ka palai. | Breathing deep of *palai* fern. |

| *Hui* | *Chorus* |
|---|---|
| Auwē ka huaʻi la. | Oh such spray. |

| | |
|---|---|
| ʻAuhea wale ana ʻoe | Listen |
| E kaʻu mea e liʻa nei | My desire |
| Mai hōʻapaʻapa mai ʻoe | Don't linger |
| O loaʻa pono kāua. | Lest we be found. |

| | |
|---|---|
| I aloha wau iāʻoe | I loved you |
| I kāu hanahana pono | Your warmth |
| Laʻi aʻe ke kaunu me ia la | Calmed passion |
| Hōʻapaʻapa i ka manaʻo. | Preventing thought. |

| **KA UA LOKU** | **POURING RAIN** |
|---|---|

Composed by Alfred U. Alohikea.

| | |
|---|---|
| Kaulana wale e ka ua o Hanalei, | You are famous, O rain of Hanalei, |
| E nihi aʻe nei i nā pali, | Creeping on the cliffs, |
| E hoʻopili ana me ka lauaʻe, | Clinging to the ferns, |
| Mehe ipo nohenohea i ka poli, | A fair sweetheart in the arms, |
| Ka hoene mai nō a ke kai | The sea sounding softly |
| Mehe ala e ʻī mai ana | As if to say |
| E hoʻi mai nō kāua la e pili, | Come back we will be as one, |
| Ka ua loku kaulana aʻo Hanalei. | Famous pouring rain of Hanalei. |

| **KAULANA NĀ PUA** | **FAMOUS ARE THE FLOWERS** |
|---|---|

The words of this *hīmeni* are bitter, yet the tune is gay (was there no feeling that the tune should reflect the mood of the words?). "Kaulana nā Pua" (famous are the children/or flowers) opposes the annexation of Hawaii to the United States and was written, according to Ethel M. Damon, by Ellen Wright Prendergast in 1893 under the title "Mele ʻAi Pohaku."

The song was considered sacred and not for dancing. Four famous chiefs are mentioned as symbols of their lands: Keawe of Hawaii, Pi'i-lani of the bays with names beginning Hono- on Maui, Mano of Kauai, and Kakuhihewa of Oahu.

Damon (1957:317) thus describes the song's composition:

"One such gifted composer, Mrs. Ellen Wright Prendergast, was sitting on an afternoon of January 1893, in the lovely garden of her father's mansion at Kapalama. Her prized guitar lay close at hand. When guests were announced, their familiar faces proved to be the troubled ones of all but two members of the Royal Hawaiian Band—on strike. 'We will not follow this new government,' they asserted. 'We will be loyal to Liliu. We will not sign the haole's paper, but will be satisfied with all that is left to us, the stones, the mystic food of our native land.' So they begged her to compose this song of rebellion, Mele 'Ai Pohaku (Stone-eating Song), called also Mele Aloha Aina (Patriots' Song).

"Long a close friend of the royal family, Ellen Prendergast found the words and music rising within her. Soon the *mele* was well known among Hawaiians. Years later, after the Royal Hawaiian Band had reassembled and again gave special afternoon concerts, it was an event when Heleluhe of the band was to sing the Mele 'Ai Pohaku. Distance and time even then were merging bitterness with legend. The origin of this Hawaiian chant has been shared with us by the composer's daughter Eleanor Prendergast."

Kaulana nā pua a'o
    Hawai'i
Kūpa'a mahope o ka 'āina
Hiki mai ka 'elele o ka loko
    'ino
Palapala 'ānunu me ka
    pākaha.

Famous are the children of
    Hawaii
Ever loyal to the land
When the evil-hearted messenger
    comes
With his greedy document of
    extortion.

Pane mai Hawai'i moku o Keawe.
Kōkua nā Hono a'o Pi'ilani.
Kāko'o mai Kaua'i o Mano
Pa'apū me ke one
    Kakuhihewa.

Hawaii, land of Keawe answers.
Pi'ilani's bays help.
Mano's Kauai lends support
And so do the sands of
    Kakuhihewa.

'A'ole 'a'e kau i ka pūlima
Maluna o ka pepa o ka 'enemi
Ho'ohui 'āina kū'ai hewa
I ka pono sivila a'o ke kanaka.

No one will fix a signature
To the paper of the enemy
With its sin of annexation
And sale of native civil rights.

'A'ole mākou a'e minamina
I ka pu'ukālā a ke
    aupuni.
Ua lawa mākou i ka pōhaku,
I ka 'ai kamaha'o o ka 'āina.

We do not value
The government's sums of
    money.
We are satisfied with the stones,
Astonishing food of the land.

Mahope mākou o Lili'u-lani
A loa'a 'ē ka pono a ka
    'āina.
(A kau hou 'ia e ke kalaunu)
Ha'ina 'ia mai ana ka puana
Ka po'e i aloha i ka
    'āina.

We back Lili'u-lani
Who has won the rights of the
    land.
(She will be crowned again)
Tell the story
Of the people who love their
    land.

## KA WILIWILIWAI     THE LAWN SPRINKLER

The words of this famous song are by Queen Lili'u-o-ka-lani. While living at Washington Place she often looked from her lanai at her neighbor's yard. When she saw there a lawn sprinkler, the first she had ever seen, she was fascinated and is said to have composed this song, the delight of bass voices.

E ka wiliwiliwai,
Ko'iawe i ka la'i.
A he aha kāu hana
E naue mālia nei?

O lawn sprinkler
Gentle shower.
What are you doing
Circling quietly?

*Hui*

Ei nei! Ei nei!
    *(bass)* Ea — ea —
Ke poahi mai nei
Āhea Āhea
    *(bass)* 'oe — 'oe
'Oe kaohi mai.

*Chorus*

You, there! You, there!
    Yes — yes —
When you spin about
Heed Heed
    You — you
Hold fast.

Oki pau 'oia ala,
Ua ninihi ka lawena.
Ku'u iki iho ho'i
I inu aku au.

How amazing,
Quiet but possessive.
Slow down a little
So I may drink.

## KE AO NANI                    THE BEAUTIFUL WORLD

This selection, delighted in by children, has long been current in Mary Kawena Pukui's family. The antithetical pairs *luna/lalo* and *uka/kai* are commonly juxtaposed in chants.

| | |
|---|---|
| I luna la, i luna,<br>Nā manu o ka lewa. | Above, above,<br>Birds of the heavens. |
| I lalo la, i lalo,<br>Nā pua o ka honua. | Below, below,<br>Flowers of the earth. |
| I uka la, i uka,<br>Nā ulu lāʻau. | In the mountains, mountains,<br>Forests. |
| I kai la, i kai,<br>Nā iʻa o ka moana. | In the sea, the sea,<br>Fish of the ocean. |
| Haʻina mai ka puana:<br>A he nani ke ao nei. | Tell the refrain:<br>This beautiful world. |

## KE KAʻUPU                    ALBATROSS

Composed by Lele-iō-Hoku, this song is about a sea bird, commonly known in English as an albatross; but how could a love song honor an albatross? (An alternate name is gooney). There are two tunes to this song, the newer one from the late 1930's. The next to the last syllable in every line is lengthened.

| | |
|---|---|
| Iā māua i hoʻolaʻi iho āi<br>Kaha ʻana ke kaʻupu i ka lāʻi<br>I laila ke aloha haʻanīpo,<br>Haʻalipo i ka poli pumehāna. | While we are at peace<br>Peacefully soars the albatross<br>And a sweetheart makes love,<br>Makes love with warm heart. |
| Kuhi au ua like me ia nēi,<br>Ka lalawe ninihi launa ʻole,<br>ʻAkahi a ʻike i ka nōe<br>Ua loha i ka wai hoʻolāna. | I thought it was so,<br>Quiet taking over, unsurpassed,<br>Never before to see such mist<br>Drooping over calmed water. |
| ʻO ka hana nipo kau ʻē ke ānu,<br>Ua maewa poniponi i ka nōe<br>Poahiahi wale ka ʻikēna.<br>Ke koni iho, koni aku,<br>   koni aʻela. | To woo in the coolness,<br>To sway in the purple mist<br>And hazy view.<br>To throb here, throb there,<br>   throb so. |
| *Hui*<br>Inā pēlā mai kāu hāna<br>Pakela ʻoi aku ka pipīʻi<br>Kāu hana ʻolu noʻeāu<br>Kohu like me Wai-ʻale-ʻāle. | *Chorus*<br>So that's your way<br>Superior but bubbling<br>Sweet clever acts<br>Like Wai-ʻale-ʻāle. |

## KILAKILA 'O HALE-A-KA-LĀ

## MAJESTIC HALE-A-KA-LĀ

This song is in praise of Maui and Hale-a-ka-lā mountain. Ka'ao'ao was a Maui chief. Kilohana is the name of the lookout on the summit of Hale-a-ka-lā and is also the name of the outside and most beautiful tapa in a layer of tapa bed covers. The slippery sands refer to the crooked paths leading down from the summit into the crater. A slight love interest in the second stanza adds to the piquancy of the song: the trotting horse is probably a young lady. Maui's favorite epithet is *Maui nō ka 'ōi*. The stanzas are usually sung slowly, and the chorus very fast. The second stanza, which is not at all about Maui, was taken from the song "Kau Ana," which dates from the 1870's.

Kauhale o Ka'ao'ao,
'Ike aku 'ia Kilohana.
Kāua i ke one he'ehe'e
Me nā alanui kike'eke'e.

Home of Ka'ao'ao,
That looks upon Kilohana.
You and I on the slippery sands
And zigzagging paths.

Kau ana la kau ana,
Kau ana kō ia ala maka
'O ua lio holo peki!
Mea 'ole kō iā ala holo!

Placing placing,
Placing his eyes
Upon that pacing horse!
Her gait is impressive!

*Hui*
Kilakila 'o Hale-a-ka-lā,
Kuahiwi nani o Maui
Ha'aheo wale 'oe Hawai'i.
Hanohano, 'o Maui nō ka 'oi.

*Chorus*
Majestic Hale-a-ka-lā,
Beautiful mountain of Maui
Prized by you, Hawaii.
Glory, Maui is the very best.

## KŌKOHI

## TO HOLD FOREVER

Composed by Lili'u-o-ka-lani, this song is also known as "Ka Wai Māpuna" (The Spring Water). Hiku in the last stanza may possibly be the Hawaiian Orpheus of that name who journeyed to the underworld, Milu, to find his sweetheart who had hung herself for love of him (Fornander, vol. 5:182-189). The red water with fiery surface refers to river waters, said to run red in beautiful fashion after storms, and perhaps signifies the turmoil of passion—but *'iliahi* might also mean "sandalwood." Is the poem a story of man's search for happiness?

Ka wai māpunapuna la
E naue mālie nei i ka la'i
Lipolipo launa 'ole la
Kauwahi 'ale 'ole iho.

Spring water
Flowing gently in the calm
Blue beyond compare
And no ripples.

| *Hui* | *Chorus* |
|---|---|
| Kōkohi i ka ʻono unahe i<br>  ka poli, | Hold the delicious moments that<br>  they may soothe the heart, |
| Ka wai olohia, | Water to and fro, |
| Paheʻe ka momoni | To sip to swallow |
| A he ʻolu ka ihona iho. | As a cool draught. |
| | |
| Lei ana Hiku i ka noe la, | Hiku's lei is the mist, |
| Hoʻohihi līhau ka lipo la. | Loved for its blue coolness. |
| Ānehe ʻoia ala e inu la | Quietly he drinks |
| Ka wai ʻula ʻili ahi. | Red water with fiery surface. |
| | |
| Iā ʻoe ka ʻuhene i ka<br>  wai | For you the joyful tune in<br>  the water |
| Ka nēnē liʻiliʻi i ke<br>  kuluaumoe, | Whispering quietly in the late<br>  night, |
| Hoʻolaʻi ka Ua-ʻula la | The Red Rain brings peace |
| Kālele nuʻa i ka palai | Resting heaped upon the ferns. |

In the queen's book in the State Archives, the meaningless refrain *ehehe* follows *kōkohi, ʻono, paheʻe,* and *momoni* in the chorus.


## KŌ MAʻI HŌʻEUʻEU                      YOUR LIVELY *MAʻI*

The *mele maʻi* are an eminently sane and healthy realization of the importance of the sexual aspects of life, and perhaps a wish for future vigor *(hōʻeuʻeu)*. They were composed shortly after the birth of the honoree, especially a well-born honoree, and were always lively and fun. In this song for King Ka-lā-kaua, the *maʻi* is named Hālala, which means overly large.

| | |
|---|---|
| Kō maʻi hōʻeuʻeu | Your lively *maʻi* |
| Hōʻekepue ana ʻoe— | That you are hiding— |
| Hōʻike i ka mea nui | Show the big thing |
| O Hālala i ka nuku manu. | Hālala to the many birds. |
| | |
| ʻO ka hana ia o Hālala— | What Hālala does— |
| Ka hapapai kīkala | Raise the hips |
| Aʻe a ka lawe aʻe ʻoe | And take you |
| A i pono iho o Hālala. | Right below Hālala. |
| | |
| Kō maʻi hoʻolalahū, | Your *maʻi* swells, |
| I kai ʻale pūnana mele, | Sea swells a nest of songs, |
| ʻO ka hope ʻoi iho ai | And finally |
| A i pehu ai kō nuku. | Your swollen mouth. |

| | |
|---|---|
| Ua pā kī'aha paha, | Take a drink perhaps, |
| Ke noenoe mai nei. | Foggy then. |
| Ha'ina mai ka puana: | Tell the refrain: |
| 'O Hālala i ka nuku manu. | Hālala and the many birds. |

| | |
|---|---|
| ### KONI AU I KA WAI | ### I THROB FOR LIQUID |

The chorus of this famous song by King Ka-lā-kaua seems to be in praise of gin, but the rest of the song, fraught with double meanings, seems to concern a love affair. *Wai* can mean any liquid, as well as fresh water. Pua-'ena is a point at Wai-a-lua Bay, Oahu. *Kini,* in the chorus, can mean "multitude" or "gin." One's birthplace is poetically called birthsands.

| | |
|---|---|
| Ho'ohihi kahi mana'o | Thoughts fancy |
| I ka 'ehu kai o Pua-'ena, | The sea spray at Pua-'ena, |
| Kai hāwanawana i ka la'i la, | Sea whispering in peace, |
| I ka la'i wale a'o Wai-a-lua. | The peace of Wai-a-lua. |

| *Hui* | *Chorus* |
|---|---|
| Koni au, koni au i ka wai, | I throb, I throb for liquid, |
| Koni au i ka wai hu'ihu'i, | I throb for cool liquid, |
| I ka wai ali'i, 'o ke kini la, | Royal liquid—gin— |
| 'Olu ai ka nohona o ka la'i. | To make life cool and peaceful. |

| | |
|---|---|
| Alia 'oe e ka 'ehu kai | Wait, O sea sprays |
| E lelehune nei i ke one, | Misting on the sands, |
| One hānau o ke kupuna la, | Birthsands of ancestors, |
| Pū'ili lau li'i o ka uka. | Small-leafed bamboo of the uplands. |

| | |
|---|---|
| 'Akahi ho'i au la 'ike | Finally I have known |
| I nā la'i 'elua; | Twofold peace; |
| 'Elua māua i ka la'i la | We two in peace |
| Wai kāpīpī i ka pali. | Liquid sprinkling on the cliff. |

| | |
|---|---|
| ### KUPA LANDING | ### COOPER LANDING |

This artful yodelling song honoring Cooper Landing at Ho'okena, Kona, Hawai'i, affords a fine example of traditional poetic techniques that will challenge any translator. Three place names are the bases of word play. Ho'okena is echoed as *ho'oheno* (to cherish). (In this translation *hō'olu'ia,* literally "cooled," is rendered "charm" so that this will suggest "cherish"; the echoism in the original is in the place name). Honomū is used as though it was *ho'omū* (to gather, flock). Kupa (from English "Cooper") is followed a few lines later by *kupa* (native) and this is contrasted in the next verse with *malihini* (visitor). Yodelling songs were popular in the late 1890's and early 1900's.

| | |
|---|---|
| Hoʻokena i ka laʻi | Hoʻokena is peaceful |
| Honomū aʻo nā manu | And the birds flock to Honomū |
| ʻIke ʻia ʻo ka lihi. | And glance about shyly. |
| Alia ʻoe a pūlale mai. | But don't you rush. |
| | |
| ʻO Kupa Landing, | Cooper Landing, |
| Hanohano i ka laʻi, | Its glorious solace, |
| Hōʻolu ʻia nō, Hoʻokena | Hoʻokena charm |
| Hoʻoheno ka manaʻo | Cherished in the thoughts |
| Nā kupa o ka ʻāina. | Of the natives of the land. |
| Hoʻōlu i ka maka o ka malihini. | Charm too in the eyes of visitors. |
| Hoʻōlu i ka maka o ka malihini. | Charm too in the eyes of visitors. |

| *Hui* | *Chorus* |
|---|---|
| Kani nei, kani nei, kani nei aʻo nā manu | Singing, singing, singing birds |
| U la, laē, u la laē u. | U la, laē, u la laē u. |

(The chorus is repeated).

## KUʻU HOME O NĀ PALI HĀULIULI

## MY HOME AND ITS GREEN CLIFFS

Composed by Mrs. Eddie Hopkins in honor of her home, Hale-kou, in Kāne-ʻohe and presented to delegate Samuel Wilder King, probably in 1939, this is the theme song of the Koʻolau-poko Hawaiian Civic Club. In the third stanza *uilani* is often sung *i o lani*.

| | |
|---|---|
| Aloha kuʻu home a i Kāne-ʻohe | Greetings to my home in Kāne-ʻohe |
| Ame nā pali hāuliuli o nā Koʻolau. | And the green cliffs of the Koʻolaus. |
| | |
| Noho aku i ka laʻi o kuʻu home | Staying in the peace of my home |
| Upu aʻe ka manaʻo nō nā hoaloha. | Bringing thoughts of friends. |
| | |
| I laila mākou uilani ai | There we find pleasure |
| Ame ka wai noenoe e pipiʻi ana. | And misty bubbling waters. |
| | |
| Hoʻokahi ka manaʻo i kualono | One thought in the mountain ranges |
| Ame ka leo aloha e hoʻokipa mai. | And the beloved voice of hospitality. |

Ha'ina 'ia mai ana ka puana:
Ame nā pali hāuliuli o nā
  Ko'olau.

Tell the refrain:
And the green cliffs of the
  Ko'olaus.

## KU'U 'ĪLIO

## MY DOG

This is a cruel missionary song for children taken from the undated book *Lira Kamalii.* The tune is either that of "London Bridge Is Falling Down" or "Yankee Doodle." The second and fourth lines in each stanza rhyme—the only examples of rhyme in this collection.

Ku'u 'īlio, ku'u 'īlio,
Wahi a ke keiki.
Holo launa, holo pū
A pau ka makahiki.

My dog, my dog,
Says the child.
Runs so friendly, runs with [me]
All year round.

*Hui*
Mai pepehi ku'u 'īlio,
Ku'u 'īlio nani,
Hoa hele, hoa
  moe,
Hoa i pā'ani.

*Chorus*
Don't beat my dog,
My pretty dog,
Friend to go with, friend to
  sleep with,
Friend to play with.

Hele pēlā kou 'īlio,
Wahi a ka 'ike.
Mea 'uku, nahu, 'ino,
Wala'au, 'āpiki.

Drive away your dog,
Says the wise one.
Fleas, bites, mean,
Noisy, naughty.

Kona 'aoa, pauwau ana
Kulikuli wale,
Mea 'aihue, ho'opau dālā,
'Ai a waiwai hale.

His bark bow wow
So noisy,
Steals, wastes money,
Eats the house's wealth.

Pono maoli ke ho'omake
Kou " 'īlio nani."
Koe ke dālā, kū'ai buke,
Waiwai nō ka lani.

Kill
Your "pretty dog."
Save money, buy books,
Wealth for heaven.

## KU'U IPO I KA HE'E
## PU'E ONE

## MY SWEETHEART IN THE
## RIPPLING HILLS OF SAND

This song was probably composed by Princess Likelike. The original name was "Ka 'Owē a ke Kai" (the murmuring of the sea). The English translation is by Ruth Lei-lani Tyau and S. H. Elbert.

Ku'u ipo i ka he'e pu'e
  one

My sweetheart in the rippling
  hills of sand

Me ke kai nehe i ka 'ili'ili,
Nipo aku i laila ka mana'o
Ua kili'opu māua i ka nahele.

With the sea rustling the pebbles,
There, the memory is impassioned
In the forest where we delighted.

Ka owē nenehe a ke kai
Hone ana i ka piko wai'olu
I laila au la 'ike
Kili'opu māua i ka nahele.

The gentle rustle of the sea
Softly in the pleasant center
Where I looked
We delighted in the forest.

Hiki 'ē mai ana ka makani
Ua hala 'ē aku e ka Pu'u-lena.
Ua lose kou chance e ke hoa:
Ua kili'opu māua i ka nahele.

The wind came first
The Pu'u-lena wind passed by.
You've lost your chance, O friend:
She and I delighted in the forest.

Eia la e maliu mai,
Eia kō aloha i 'ane'i.
Hiki mai ana i ka pō nei.
Ua kili'opu māua i ka nahele.

Here, please listen,
Here, your lover is here.
He came last night.
We delighted in the forest.

## KU'U LEI

## MY LEI

This is a name song composed by Mary Kawena Pukui for her grandson, La'akea, shortly after his birth on November 8, 1949. The "many birds" are admiring people.

'Ohu'ohu wale au i ku'u lei
    onaona,
Ku'u lei ho'ohie o nā kau a kau.
Au mai nā maka o ka nui manu
I ku'u wehi nani e lei mau
    nei.

I wear my fragrant
    lei,
My lei cherished in all seasons.
The eyes of many birds behold
My beautiful ornament to be
    worn forever as a lei.

*Hui*

Ku'u lei, lei onaona,
Māpu ho'oheno nei i ku'u
    poli.
Ku'u lei, lei ho'ohie,
Ku'u wehi nani e lei mau
    nei.

*Chorus*

My lei, my fragrance,
Wafted perfume to cherish in
    my heart.
My lei, delightful lei,
My beautiful ornament to be
    worn forever as a lei.

Haku 'ia ku'u lei
E nā lima no'eau
A wili 'ia me ke aloha na'u e
    lei.
Pūlama iho au a hi'ipoi mau
I ku'u wehi nani e lei mau
    nei.

My lei is woven
By skillful hands
Interwoven with love for me to
    wear as a lei.
I cherish and hold forever
My beautiful ornament to be worn
    forever as a lei.

71

## KUʻU LEI PŪPŪ

## MY SHELL LEI

The words, music, and English translation of this hula were written by Mary Kawena Pukui for the Lei Day pageant directed by her friend, Rosalie Montgomery, at the University of Hawaii in 1952. Mrs. Montgomery had songs for many islands, but needed a song about the beautiful Niihau shell leis. An informant says that the Niihau people like the song so much that during the years they have added more than a score of stanzas. This fondness for long songs is typical of old Hawaii, and remains on Niihau.

| | |
|---|---|
| Mahalo aʻe au i ka nani | I admire the beauty |
| O kuʻu lei pūpū poina ʻole | Of my unforgettable shell lei |
| | |
| I kui ʻia me ka nui noʻeau | Strung together with great skill |
| I wehi hoʻohie nō kuʻu kino. | Into an ornament for me to wear. |
| | |
| Mai nā nalu a ka lihi ʻae one | From the waves to the edge of the sands |
| Nā pūpū o ka pae ʻana mai. | My sea shells come to land. |
| | |
| ʻOhi au a kui a lawa pono | I gathered and strung to completeness |
| I lei kāhiko nā ka makemake. | The lovely lei that I desire. |
| | |
| Haʻina ʻia mai ana ka puana | This is the end of my praise |
| Ka wehi hoʻohie o kuʻu kino. | Of the lovely adornment I wear. |

## KUʻU PUA I PAOA-KA-LANI

## MY FLOWER AT PAOA-KA-LANI

Composed, by Queen Liliʻu-o-ka-lani during her imprisonment in ʻIo-lani Palace, as a name song (*mele inoa*) perhaps for the son of Evelyn Townsend Wilson, an intimate of the queen who went into voluntary imprisonment with her. The son was John Wilson, later mayor of Honolulu. The queen was not allowed newspapers, but John sent them in with flowers, presumably from her own garden at Ulu-hai-malama, an area now known as Liliʻu-o-ka-lani Park. Paoa-ka-lani (fragrance of the royal chief) was the name of the queen's home near the street with that name in Waikiki. This song shows how English words were used with Hawaiian grammar.

| | |
|---|---|
| E ka gentle breeze e waft mai nei | O gentle breeze waft hither |
| Hoʻohāliʻaliʻa mai ana iaʻu | And remind me |
| ʻO kuʻu sweet never fading flower | Of my sweet never fading flower |
| I bloom i ka uka o Paoa-ka-lani. | That has bloomed in the depths of Paoa-ka-lani. |

72

|  |  |
|---|---|
| *Hui* | *Chorus* |

'Ike mau i ka nani o nā
    pua
I uka o Ulu-hai-malama.
'A'ole na'e ho'i e like
Me ku'u pua la'i o
    Paoa-ka-lani.

See forever the beauty of the
    flowers
Inland at Ulu-hai-malama.
None the equal
Of my gentle flower of
    Paoa-ka-lani.

Lahilahi kona mau hi'ona
With softest eyes as black as jet,
Pink cheeks so delicate of hue
I ulu i ka uka o
    Paoa-ka-lani.

Dainty face
With softest eyes as black as jet,
Pink cheeks so delicate of hue
Growing in the depths of
    Paoa-ka-lani.

Nanea 'ia mai ana ku'u aloha.
E ka gentle breeze e waft mai
    nei,
O come to me ka'u mea li'a nei
I ulu i ka uka o
    Paoa-ka-lani.

My love delights.
O gentle breeze, waft
    hither,
O come to me my beloved
Growing in the depths of
    Paoa-ka-lani.

## LĀNA'I

The words are by Mary Keliiaukai Robins, who lived on many islands with her lighthouse-keeper husband. The music is by Johnny Noble. The *hala* in the song refers to pineapples *(hala Kahiki)* rather than to pandanus *(hala),* which is rare on Lanai.

Hanohano ka inoa o Lāna'i
Lei ana i ka pua o ke kauna'oa.

Distinguished name Lāna'i
Wearing the *kauna'oa* flower lei.

'Ōlelo kauoha nā ku'u aloha,
Hina wau i ka hewa mamuli o'u.

My beloved speaks a command,
I fall in sin myself.

Ua ola nā kini o ka 'āina
I ka hui hana hala a'o ke
    kaona.

The people of the land live
Due to the *hala* company work
    of the town.

Ke moani mai nā 'ala, e ka hala,
Ke hea mai nei ia'u e kipa.

Fragrance wafts hither, O *hala,*
Calling me to visit.

Hea aku nō wau e ō mai 'oe,
Lei ana Lāna'i i ke kauna'oa.

I call and you answer,
Lāna'i wears the *kauna'oa* lei.

## LEI 'AWAPUHI          GINGER LEI

Composed by Mekia Ke-alaka'i, one of the boys taken from the Industrial School by the German band leader Henry Berger;

Ke-alaka'i later became band leader. The melody is said to have occurred to Ke-alaka'i on a train ride to the Chicago World Fair of the 1890's. The train broke down and the Hawaiians got off to pick wild poppies; this inspired Ke-alaka'i to write the music. He already had the words.

He leo nō ka ipo ka'u i lohe iho,
Na'u e kākele a mau ia pua
Ua ho'oholo like 'ia e ka naulu
E kui i wehi nō ka liko.

I have heard the sweetheart's voice,
I have cast to catch this flower
Moving like the rain
To string as a lei with festive buds.

Ho'ohihi wale nō ke aloha i laila
Ia pua i mōhala i ka 'iu.
Na'u e ke aloha e kui a lawa,
Me a'u kou lei 'awapuhi.

Delighted love there
This flower that opens far away.
My love, you are securely bound to me,
Your ginger lei to me.

*Hui*

Lei 'awapuhi, lei hiki ahiahi,
Hoa pili o maile-lau-li'i
Lana mālie iho ho'i ka mana'o
Me ka nani lei 'awapuhi.

*Chorus*

Ginger lei, lei that comes in the evening,
Close friend of small-leafed-*maile*
Thinking with calm hope
Of the beauty of ginger lei.

## MAI HŌ'EU'EU MAI 'OE

## DON'T HURRY

This song mentions the mists of Ka'ala, the highest mountain on Oahu, the winds called Mālua and Kiu, and the land shells that the Hawaiians believe sing gently, especially late at night.

'Auhea wale ana 'oe,
Uhiwai o Ka'ala
I pili me ka Mālua
Ka makani o ka 'āina.

Listen,
Mist of Ka'ala
Coming with the Mālua
Wind of the land.

*Hui*

Mai hō'eu'eu mai 'oe
I ka wai ua lana mālie.
E kakali mālie 'oe
A la'i pono ka makani.

*Chorus*

Don't hurry
Into water that appears to float calmly.
Wait quietly
Until the wind settles down.

Ho'okahi a'u mea uluhua
Ka makani anu la he Kiu

My only worry
Is the cold Kiu wind

Houhou ana i ka ‘ili
Konikoni i ka iwihilo.

Piercing my skin
And quivering my thigh bones.

‘A‘ole i piliwi ‘ia
Leo hone o ke
  kāhuli
Hone ana i ka pō la‘i
I ke kulukulu aumoe?

Can you believe
The sweet voice of the land
  shells
That sing on calm nights
At late hours?

## MAIKA‘I KAUA‘I      KAUAI BEAUTY

This well-known song is said to have been based on a chant and to have been composed by Ka-pa‘akea, the father of Ka-lā-kaua, in honor of Pau-ahi Bishop's adopted child, Ke-ola-o-ka-lani (the life of the royal chief), who died at the age of seven months. The original chant may have honored Ka-umu-ali‘i, the Kauai chief who finally acknowledged Kamehameha's sovereignty. Henry Waia‘u composed the music when he was choir director of the Lihu‘e Hawaiian Church on Kauai. With this composition, then called "Lei i ka Mokihana," his choir won a Congregational competition in Honolulu. Namolo-kama is a waterfall in Hanalei.

Maika‘i wale nō Kaua‘i
Hemolele wale i ka mālie.
Kuahiwi nani, Wai‘ale‘āle,
Lei ana i ka mokihana.

So very beautiful is Kaua‘i
So perfect in the calm.
Pretty mountain, Wai‘ale‘āle,
Wears the *mokihana* lei.

Hanohano wale ‘o Hanalei
I ka ua nui hō‘eha
  ‘ili
I ka wai o ‘u‘inakolo
I ka poli o Namolokama.

So glorious is Hanalei
With the great rain that pains
  the skin
And the rustling water
In the heart of Namolokama.

Maika‘i nō Kaua‘i,
Hemolele i ka mālie.
Kuahiwi Wai‘ale‘āle
Lei ana i ka mokihana.

So beautiful is Kaua‘i,
So perfect in the calm.
Mount Wai‘ale‘āle
Wears the *mokihana* lei.

## MAKALAPUA      PROFUSE BLOOM

The words to this song honoring Lili‘u-o-ka-lani were taken by Konia, apparently Lili‘u's foster mother and the mother of Pau-ahi Bishop, from an old chant. The music, by Eliza Holt, was adapted from the tune "Would I Were With Thee." Lili‘u thought that chants were going out of fashion, and asked that music be written for a song. Lili‘u's two names, Lili‘u (smarting) and Ka-maka-‘eha (the sore eye) were given at her birth by the regent, Kīnaʻu, who was suffering from sore eyes. (Hawaiians dated a child's birth by naming the child for an important event happening at that time—even one's own sore eyes. This custom was useful before dates were written, but still continues.)

This is an Oahu song. In stanza 3 are Mount Kaʻala and Hale-ʻauʻau (bath house), a gulch at Wai-a-lua. In stanza 4 is Kekele (damp), a place below Nuʻu-anu Pali famous for *hala* (pandanus) trees. Waʻahila is a rain at Manoa and Nuʻu-anu.

| | |
|---|---|
| ʻO makalapua ulu māhiehie | Profuse bloom growing as a delight |
| ʻO ka lei o Ka-maka-ʻeha, | And lei for Ka-maka-ʻeha, |
| Nō Ka-maka-ʻeha ka lei nā Liʻa Wāhine, | For Ka-maka-ʻeha the lei of the forest goddesses, |
| Nā wāhine kīhene pua. | The ladies with baskets of flowers. |

| *Hui* | *Chorus* |
|---|---|
| E lei hoʻi, e Liliʻu-lani e. | Wear a lei, O Liliʻu-lani. |
| E lei hoʻi, e Liliʻu-lani e. | Wear a lei, O Liliʻu-lani. |

| | |
|---|---|
| Haʻihaʻi pua kamani paukū pua kī | Pluck *kamani* flowers to link with ti flowers |
| I lei hoʻowehiwehi no ka wahine | As a lei to adorn the lady |
| E walea ai ka wao kele | Beloved by the forest glens |
| I nā liko iō mauna (na) hele. | And the buds in the mountain greenery. |

| | |
|---|---|
| Lei Kaʻala i ka ua o ka naulu | Kaʻala wears a lei of rain and showers |
| Hoʻoluʻe iho la i lalo o Hale-ʻauʻau, | Pouring down on Hale-ʻauʻau, |
| Ka ua lei kōkōʻula i ke pili | Rainbow mist that is a lei on *pili* grass |
| I pilia ka mauʻu nēnē me ke kupukupu. | Where *nēnē* grass grows close to *kupukupu* ferns. |

| | |
|---|---|
| Lei aku la i ka hala o Kekele, | Wearing a lei of *hala* fruit of Kekele, |
| Nā hala moe ipo o Malailua | *Hala* of Malailua that sweethearts dream of |
| Ua māewa wale i ke oho o ke kāwelu | Swaying freely amid *kāwelu* grasses |
| Nā lei kamakahala o ka ua Waʻahila. | *Kamakahala* flower leis of Waʻahila rain. |

76

## MANU 'Ō'Ō                    HONEY-EATER

In Hawaiian poetry the birds that sip *lehua* honey and the rain that pelts *lehua* leaves are linked romantically. In this *himeni* the girl is compared to the *manu 'ō'ō,* the nearly extinct black honey-eater whose yellow feathers were used for featherwork. The lover likens himself to the *lehua* blossoms. In the last stanza the girl is the *lehua*-sounding rain of Hilo and the man the *lehua* of Hanakahi, a place on the Hāmākua side of Hilo noted for profound peace (Emerson 1965:60-61).

'O ka manu 'ō'ō i mālama,
A he nani kou hulu ke lei
   'ia.
Mūkīkī ana 'oe i ka pua lehua
Kāhea ana 'oe i ka nui manu.

Precious honey-eater,
Your feathers are beautiful
   woven into a lei.
You sip *lehua* flowers
And call other birds.

*Hui*
Hō mai, 'oni mai
Kō aloha ma nēia
Kīhene lehua.

*Chorus*
Come, fly hither
To your beloved
*Lehua* cluster.

Nō Hilo e ka ua
   Kani-lehua,
Popohe lehua ai Hanakahi.
Ho'okahi a'u mea nui aia 'oe
'O kou aloha ua hiki mai.

You *lehua*-sounding rain are
   from Hilo,
Shapely *lehua* at Hanakahi.
The one I love is you
Your lover has come.


## MOANA-LUA

This song, arranged by David Nape, exemplifies two characteristics of Hawaiian songs: that of storytelling, and of traveling about from place to place. (For some of the many traveling songs in Emerson, 1909, see pp. 60-63, 85-87, 203.)

The trip of pleasure, presumably by a girl, starts with a breakdown (of a carriage?) at Moana-lua; then moves to Ka-hau-iki (the town side of Ft. Shafter) where the liquor bottle is uncorked, apparently to remain so over the plains of Ka-lihi; thence to Ka-iwi-'ula (site of the Bishop Museum), where the teller tilts over from drink; to Ka-pā-lama (now Pā-lama); to Ke-one-'ula (site of Kau-maka-pili Church); and to Leleo, Ha'alili-a-manu, Ka-pu'u-kolo, Ka-nēkina (all near Hotel Street and Nu'u-anu Stream), where the girl rides a merry-go-round with an *ulua* fish (sweetheart); finally at nearby Ka-manu-wai the girl woos underage youngsters whom she'll hurt. The *noni (Morinda citrofolia)* fruit is very bitter.

(*Ulua* fish were substitutable as human sacrifices probably because *ulu* means "possessed or inspired by a god." Even after human sacrifices ceased, a man might be called an *ulua*. This is how we know that a female is talking.)

| | |
|---|---|
| I Moana-lua ha'i ke 'au, | At Moana-lua the shaft breaks, |
| I Ka-hau-iki hemo ka 'umoki. | At Ka-hau-iki take out the cork. |
| | |
| 'O ke kula loa ho'i o Ka-lihi, | The long plain of Ka-lihi, |
| 'O Ka-iwi-'ula kīki'i pau. | At Ka-iwi-'ula tilt back. |
| | |
| 'O Ka-pā-lama lo'i laiki, | At Ka-pā-lama rice patches, |
| I Ke-one-'ula malu ke kiawe. | At Ke-one-'ula, *kiawe* shade. |
| | |
| 'O Leleo, a he loko wai, | At Leleo, a pond, |
| Ha'alili-a-manu honi kāua. | At Ha'alili-a-manu, we kiss. |
| | |
| 'O Ka-pu'u-kolo, i Ka-nēkina | At Ka-pu'u-kolo and Ka-nēkina |
| Holo lio lā'au me ka | Ride a merry-go-round with an |
|    ulua. |    *ulua* fish. |
| | |
| 'O Ka-manu-wai moa li'ili'i, | At Ka-manu-wai, little chicks, |
| Hauna ke kai 'eha 'oe | Strong-smelling soup and I hurt |
|    ia'u. |    you. |
| | |
| He aha 'ē ke kumu o ka 'eha | What's the reason for the |
|    'ana? |    pain? |
| 'Ōno'onou 'ia i ka hua noni. | A *noni* fruit forced in. |
| | |
| Auwē 'eha 'ino i ku'u kīkala, | *Auwē,* how my hips hurt, |
| Pehea la ia e lewa hou ai? | How then to wander anew? |

## MOLOKA'I NUI A HINA     GREAT MOLOKA'I OF HINA

In this popular paean to the island of Moloka'i are references to the mythical mother of the island (Hina), an ancient chief (Pi'i-lani), the island lei *(kukui),* and two place names (Lani-kāula, Hālawa). Linking of height with superiority and with the highly born is more frequent in Hawaiian symbolic language than in English, and here four references to height *(po'okela, piko, ki'eki'e, heke)* attest the general superiority of the island. Poetic echoism is represented by *lupalupa lau lipo,* with only six distinctive sounds comprising a sequence of fifteen sounds. As is common in Hawaiian, praise of a place is more piquant if there are thinly veiled references to attractive denizens therein; here two flowers, the *kukui* and the crown, are romantically linked to the singer.

| | |
|---|---|
| Ua nani nā hono a | How beautiful are the bays of |
|    Pi'i-lani |    Pi'i-lani |

I ke kū kilakila i ka
  'ōpua.
'O ku'u pua kukui, aia i
  Lani-kāula,
'O ka hene wai 'olu lana
  mālie.

That stand majestically by the
  billowy clouds.
My *kukui* flower is at
  Lani-kāula,
Where water flows with cool and
  soothing rustle.

### Hui

Ua like nō a like la —
Me ku'u one hānau,
Ke po'okela i ka piko o nā
  kuahiwi,
Me Moloka'i nui a Hina,
'Āina i ka wehiwehi,
E ho'i nō au e pili.
E ka makani ē, e pā mai me
  ke aheahe,
'Auhea ku'u pua kalaunu.
E ka makani ē, e pā mai me
  ke aheahe,
'Auhea ku'u pua kalaunu.

Ki'eki'e Halawa i ke alo o
  nā pali,
Ka heke nō ia i ka'u 'ike.
Lupalupa lau lipo i ke oho o
  ka palai,
Ma ku'u poli mai 'oe e
  ho'oheno nei.

### Chorus

Alike —
The sands of my birth,
The tops of all
  mountains,
And Hina's great Moloka'i,
Festive land,
May I return to stay.
O wind, blow
  gently,
Heed, my crown flower.
O wind, blow
  gently,
Heed, my crown flower.

Halawa is high amidst the
  cliffs,
Highest I have ever seen.
And here are lush leaves and
  green fern fronds,
So you are loved within my
  arms.

## NĀ ALI'I

## THE CHIEFS

Composed by Samuel Kuahiwi, this was an appeal to the Hawaiian
societies to honor the departed chiefs, especially Kamehameha I. In
the *hīmeni* are two famous sayings. The first is Kamehameha I's law
of the splintered paddle (*māmala hoe*) that guaranteed the safety of
women, children, and the infirm upon the highways. The second is
Kamehameha III's 1843 statement at Ka-wai-a-Ha'o Church that has
become the motto of Hawai'i. The stirring tune and fine words are
justly beloved by Hawaiians and the entirety is an expression of
respect and love for the Hawaiian heritage.

Aloha nā 'ahahui o nā ali'i,
Nā ali'i mai nā kūpuna mai.
E pa'a i nā 'ōlelo kaulana,
E hele a moe i ke ala.

Hail societies of chieftains,
Chieftains from our ancestors.
Remember the famous saying,
Go and sleep upon the byways.

Hū wale a'e nā ho'omana'o 'ana
Nō nā ali'i kaulana.
Ua pau, ua hala lākou,
A koe nō nā pua.
Ua pau, ua hala lākou,
A koe nō nā pua.

Memories come
Of the famous chiefs.
They are gone, they have passed,
And their flowers survive.
They are gone, they have passed,
And their flowers survive.

E lei i ka lei ha'aheo o
    Hawai'i,
Ka wehi ho'i o nā ali'i i hala.
E pa'a ka mana'o me ka lōkahi
E mau ke ea o ka 'āina i ka
    pono.
He ali'i 'o ka lani, ua kaulana
Ka Napoliona o ka Pākīpika.
E lei i ka wehi ha'aheo o
    Hawai'i,
Nā hulu mamo like 'ole.
E lei i ka wehi ha'aheo o
    Hawai'i,
Nā hulu mamo like 'ole.

Wear the cherished leis of
    Hawai'i,
Adornment of departed chiefs.
May all unite in recalling
That the life of the land is
    perpetuated in righteousness.
Royal chief, famous
Napoleon of the Pacific.
Wear the cherished adornments of
    Hawaii,
The *mamo* feather leis.
Wear the cherished adornments of
    Hawaii,
The *mamo* feather leis.

'Imi nui 'o Maleka a lōli'i
Ka wehi ho'i o nā ali'i i
    hala
'A'ole nō na'e e like aku
Me ka mea no'eau ke kupuna.
He ali'i 'o ka lani ua kaulana,
Ke 'ahi-kananā o ka Pākīpika.
Nāna nō i ulupā nā pae moku.
A pau malalo ona.
Nāna nō i ulupā nā pae moku.
A pau malalo.

America seeks our welfare.
The adornment of departed
    chiefs
Not the same
As the ancestors' wisdom.
Chief royal and famous,
Fierce tuna of the Pacific.
When he struck the island group.
All were subdued.
When he struck the island group.
All were subdued.

## NĀ HALA O NAUE          THE PANDANUS OF NAUE

This song by J. Ka-hinu honors Ka-lele-o-nā-lani (the flight of the royal ones), a name taken by Queen Emma after the death of her husband, Kamehameha IV, in 1863. A year earlier her infant son had died, and her husband had given her the name Ka-lele-o-ka-lani (the flight of the royal one). Praise of trees, flowers, birds, and places (Naue and Hā'ena on Kauai) was a way of honoring a beloved or important person. The Hono- bays were six Maui bays with names beginning Hono- and ruled by Chief Pi'i-lani. Note the linked terminals: ha'ena/'ena, i laila/ i laila, 'ala/ke 'ala. Years after the song was composed, *'eā 'eā* in each verse was replaced by *toumi toumi,* which might be translated "press gently," but is probably merely a pleasant refrain.

Nani wale nā hala, 'eā, 'eā
O Naue i ke kai, 'eā, 'eā.

So beautiful are the pandanus
Of Naue by the sea.

Ke 'oni a'ela, 'eā, 'eā
Pili mai Hā'ena, 'eā, 'eā.

Moving there
At Hā'ena.

'Ena aku nā maka, 'eā, 'eā
'O nā manu i ka pua, 'eā, 'eā.

Fiery eyes,
Birds upon the flowers.

A 'ike i ka lehua, 'eā, 'eā
Miki'ala i laila, 'eā, 'eā.

See *lehua*
Alert.

I laila nō au, 'eā, 'eā
Me ka mana'o pū, 'eā, 'eā.

There am I
In thought.

Nani wale ka nahele, 'eā, 'eā
I puia 'ala, 'eā, 'eā.

The forest is beautiful
Drenched with fragrance.

Ke 'ala laua'e, 'eā, 'eā
'O ka pua mokihana, 'eā, 'eā.

Fragrance of ferns
And *mokihana* flowers.

Oni aku nā Hono-, 'eā, 'eā,
O ua la'i lani, 'eā, 'eā.

The Hono- bays appear
Heavenly peace.

'O ko'u lei ia, 'eā, 'eā
O ua la'i lani, 'eā, 'eā.

She is my lei
And regal peace.

Ha'ina 'ia mai, 'eā,'eā:
'O Ka-lele-o-nā-lani, 'eā, 'eā.

Tell the refrain:
The-flight-of-the-royal-ones.

Naue in a chant in Emerson (1965:56, 212) probably refers to Puna, Hawaii, rather than to Kauai; both are famous for pandanus:

Nō Naue ka hala,
Nō Puna ka wahine
Nō ka lua nō i Kī-lau-ea.

In Naue is pandanus,
In Puna is a woman
Of the pit in Kī-lau-ea.

### NĀ KA PUEO                FROM THE *PUEO*

The *Pueo-kahi* was a ship named for a place near Hāna, Maui, which had been named for an owl demigod (*pueo,* owl). Perhaps the song was composed by a sailor. Honolulu harbor was called Māmala; note the play on words with *mālama.*

Nā ka Pueo-kahi ke aloha,
Nēnē 'au kai o Maui.

Love from the *Pueo-kahi,*
The Maui goose that sails the sea.

Kōwelo kō hae Hawai'i
Ma ka 'ilikai a'o Māmala.

Your Hawaiian flag waves
Over the sea at Māmala.

Mālama 'ia iho ke aloha
I kuleana na'u e hiki aku ai.

Keep your love
And I have the right to come.

Ha'ina 'ia mai ka puana:
Nā ka Pueo-kahi ke aloha.

Tell the refrain:
Love from the *Pueo-kahi.*

## NĀ 'ONO O KA 'ĀINA    DELICACIES OF THE LAND

This song glorifies the deliciousness of fish, but there is probably a romantic *kaona* throughout. The Lanai people say that the composer was Abraham Kauila, a Lanai cowboy; this song is a Lanai favorite.

The fish names are not translated. Most fishermen prefer to say *mā'i'i'i* rather than *Acanthurus, kole* rather than surgeon fish, *'ōpelu* rather than mackerel scad, and *akule* rather than goggle-eyed scad.

Nā 'ono o ka 'āina
Hāli'ali'a wale mai nō
'O ka mā'i'i'i me ke kole
Ma ka onaona o nā Kona.
Mai apakau i kā ha'i
O nahu pū me ka unahi.
'Ai nō nā ke kino pono'ī,
Lawe a'e nō a 'ike i ka 'ono.

Delicacies of the land
Remember fondly
*Mā'i'i'i* and *kole* fish
The fragrance of the Konas.
Don't grab someone else's
Or bite the scales.
Eat the true flesh,
Take and taste the delicacy.

Ka 'ono i'a a nā kūpuna,
I'a kaulana o ka 'āina.
He 'ono i ka 'ai maka i ka
    lomilomi
He 'ono nō i ka nahunahu pū.
Mai kali a pau nā niho
O hala 'ē ka
    Pu'ulena.
'O ka wā keia 'o ka 'ono la
A i 'ike i ke kuhikuhinia.

Fish delicacies of the ancients,
Famous fish of the land.
Delicious to eat raw or
    lomilomi
Delicious to chew.
Don't wait until teeth are gone
Or the Pu'ulena wind has
    passed by.
Now is the delicious time
To savor rich fat.

'O ka māikoiko ke
    pala,
'O ka 'ina me ke ka'ukama kai,
'O ka 'ōpelu me ke akule,
A he nui wale aku nā 'ono.
Mai apakau na'e i kā ha'i
O nahu pū me ka unahi.
'Ai nō nā ke kino pono'ī,
Lawe a'e nō a 'ike i ka 'ono.

The *māikoiko* fish slightly
    mellow,
Sea urchins and sea cucumbers,
*'Ōpelu* and *akule,*
My how delicious.
Don't grab someone else's
Or bite the scales.
Eat the true flesh,
Take and taste the delicacy.

## NIU HAOHAO    YOUNG COCONUTS

Composed by Bina Mossman. The last line tells what the song is about. Or does it?

Nā wai, nā wai nō 'oe a'e pakele aku (pakele aku)?

Who, who will save you (save)?

I ka wai, i ka wai o ka niu, o ka niu haohao (niu haohao),

The water, water of the coconut, the young coconut (young coconut),

He ma'ū, ma'ū, ma'ū i ka pu'u ke moni

Wet, wet, wet the throat and swallow

Kaomi, kaomi mālie a'e i ke kīleo

Down, down gently down past the uvula

E pakika (e pakika), e pahe'e (e pahe'e),

Slither (slither), slide (slide),

E pakika i kahi wai o ka 'āina nui.

Slide liquor from the continent.


## OLD PLANTATION

The words are by Mary Jane Montano and the music by David Nape. This *hīmeni* honors the old Ward estate and coconut plantation established in 1880 at King and Ward streets, now the site of the Honolulu International Center. A water wheel stood near King Street. The owner of the property for many years was Curtis P. Ward from the southern United States, famous for its old plantations. The less-used Hawaiian name of the song is "Ku'u Home" (my home).

Pua wale mai nō ke aloha
Ka paia puia i ke
    'ala
I ka wai hu'ihu'i aniani
Ko'iawe ka huila wai.
Aia i laila ka 'i'ini
Ka 'ano'i a ko'u pu'uwai.

Love flowers
In the bower suffused with
    fragrance
And whose cool clear water
Is a water wheel's shower.
There desire
Is cherished in my heart.


*Hui*
Old plantation nani
    'oe,
Home pumehana i ke aloha,
I ka 'olu o ka niu, i ka poli
    o ke onaona.

*Chorus*
Old plantation, how beautiful
    you are,
Home warm with love,
Cool coconut grove and in its
    heart only sweetness.

# PA'AHANA

This is an example of the old type of song that tells a story. Pā'ahana (busy) was a girl mistreated by her stepmother. She ran into the hills above Wahi-a-wā and lived on river shrimps and guava until she was discovered by a cowboy and taken back to Mānana, the present site of Pearl City.

He inoa kēia nō Pa'ahana,
Kaikamahine noho kuahiwi.

This is a name song for Pa'ahana,
The girl who lived in the hills.

Na'u i noho aku ia wao kele,
Ia uka 'iu'iu
    Wahi-a-wā.

I lived in the rain forests,
The distant uplands of
    Wahi-a-wā.

'Opae 'oeha'a o ke kahawai,
'O ka hua o ke kuawa ka'u 'ai ia.

Clawed shrimps of the streams,
Guava fruits my food.

Mai kuhi mai 'oe ka makuahine,
A he pono keia e noho nei.

Don't think about the mother,
I live here and am glad.

'O kahi mu'umu'u pili i ka 'ili,
'O ka lau lā'ī ko'u kapa ia.

A single mu'umu'u clings my skin,
My blankets are ti leaves.

Pīlali kukui kau lā'au
Lau o ke pili ko'u hale ia.

*Kukui* gum on the trees
And *pili* grass my home.

I hume iho au ma ka pūhaka
I nalo iho ho'i kahi hilahila.

I bind my loins
And hide my private parts.

I ho'i iho ho'i au e pe'e
'Ike 'ē 'ia mai e ka 'enemi.

I came and hid
To be seen by the enemy.

Lawe 'ia aku au a i Mānana
Māka'ika'i 'ia e ka malihini.

I was taken to Mānana
And visited by strangers.

Ha'ina 'ia mai ana ka puana:
He mele he inoa nō Pa'ahana.

Tell the refrain:
A song, a name for Pa'ahana.


## PALISA                    PARIS

This hula is said to have been composed by a youngster, ill in the hospital, who had just seen a moving picture which showed the places mentioned in the song. Some informants say the boy had leprosy. The song was popular at the California Fair of 1915.

Palisa aku nei au
I ka lele pāluna
Pōniuniu.

I'm in Paris
Flying in a balloon
Dizzily.

84

| | |
|---|---|
| Nanea i ka lele a ka pāluna. | Fun to fly in a balloon. |
| 'Alawa iho 'oe | You look down |
| Ani ka makani. | And the wind blows by. |
| | |
| 'Inia aku nei au | I'm in India |
| I ke kau 'elepani | Riding on an elephant |
| Ihu peleleu. | With a long nose. |
| | |
| 'Aikupika aku nei au | I'm in Egypt |
| I ke kau kāmelo | Riding a camel |
| Holo kapakahi. | Running sideways. |
| | |
| I Palisa aku nei au, | I'm in Paris, |
| Kūlanakauhale | City |
| Nani lua 'ole. | Beautiful without an equal. |
| | |
| 'Alawa iho 'oe i kahi ki'i kole. | Look at my dolly. |
| Aia ma ka 'ao'ao | On its side |
| Kona kī 'oni. | A key to make it move. |
| | |
| Ha'ina 'ia mai ana ka puana | Tell the story |
| Kūlanakauhale | Of the city |
| Nani lua 'ole | Beautiful without an equal. |

## PUA LILIA        LILY

Composed by Alfred U. Alohikea.

| | |
|---|---|
| 'Auhea wale 'oe e ka ua | Heed, O rain |
| Ke nihi a'e nei i nā pali. | Creeping on the cliffs. |
| Ka helena o ia pua i 'ako 'ia, | Apparently this flower has been plucked, |
| He popohe mai nei ia uka, | Shapely forest, |
| Ia uka ho'i au e walea ai | Forest wherein I delight |
| Me he 'ala onaona o ku'u pua. | With the soft fragrance of my flower. |
| He pua 'oe na'u i lei mau ai, | You are a flower for me to wear as a lei forever, |
| Ke 'ala ku'u pua lilia. | Fragrance of my lily. |

## PUIA KA NAHELE        FOREST IMBUED WITH FRAGRANCE

Composed by Princess Lili'u-o-ka-lani in 1868. Kau-ka-'iu (placed on high) is a place name. Birds may refer to sweethearts. The *'iwi* is the scarlet honey-creeper, whose feathers were used in featherwork. *Iwa* following *'iwi* is probably a garble for *hiwa* (cherished).

Nō Kau-ka-'iu i ka wao
Ke ano hāli'ali'a
Ke kau 'ana mai 'o ka 'āluna
   ahiahi
Hiki pū mai me ke aloha.

For Kau-ka-'iu in the uplands
Silent thoughts
As the evening
   falls
And love comes.

*Hui*

Puia ka nahele, māpu mai ke
   'ala
Ka nahele (nahele) 'ona 'ia e
   nā manu
E ka 'iwi iwa maka onaona,
Ho'i mai kāua e pili nō
   (e pili).

*Chorus*

Forest imbued with fragrance,
   wafted sweetness
Of the forest that infatuates
   the birds
Of sweet-eyed cherished *'iwi*,
Come back to be with me
   (to be with me).

Noe wale mai nō ka nahele,
He ua nihi pali
Luhe ka lau o ka palai
'Elo i ka ua Wa'ahila.

The forest is misty,
Rain is creeping on the cliff
And fern fronds are drooping
Wet by the Wa'ahila rain.

## PULUPĒ NEI 'ILI I KE ANU

## MY SKIN IS WET AND COLD

In Hawaiian songs, wet and cold may signify love. Lani-huli is the mountain to the west of the Pali gap. *Buenos* is probably short for Spanish *buenas noches,* good night. Compare *bonito* in "Hālona."

Uluwehi ka luna i
   Lani-huli
Pulupē i ka nihi a ka ua.
A'o 'oe, a'o wau i laila
I ke onaona o ka nahele.

Mount Lani-huli is green with
   growth
Wet in the creeping rain.
You and I are there
In the fragrant forest.

*Hui*

Pulupē nei 'ili i ke anu,
A he anu mea 'ole i ka mana'o
'O ka 'ike iā'oe, e ke aloha,
Ho'i pono ka 'i'ini iā loko.

*Chorus*

My skin is wet and cold,
Cold does not matter
Because to see you, beloved,
Desire mounts within.

I laila li'a ka mana'o
Pūku'i i ke anu a ka
   ua,

To think is to wish
To nestle away from the cold
   and rain,

Kolonahe aʻela i ka
  uka
Me ke kēhau o ka nahele.

And amid the gentle breezes in
  the uplands
And the dew of the forest.

E maliu mai ʻoe, e ke aloha,
Kuʻu dear love o ka pō laʻi.
Buenos once more e ke hoa,
Koʻu time huli hoʻi kāua.

Listen, my beloved,
My dear love of quiet nights.
*Buenos* once more, my dear,
Time for us to go back.

## PUNA PAIA ʻAʻALA

## PUNA'S FRAGRANT GLADES

Composed by Princess Liliʻu-o-ka-lani. Puna, Hawaii, is associated with fragrance, especially of pandanus, and fragrance is associated alike with noble birth and love making. (See "Nā Hala o Naue.") The chorus in this song is sung as indicated below, but *kilihea* and *nawela* should probably be *kilihē* (drenched) and *nawele* (tracery).

Iā Puna paia ʻaʻala
Pili mau nā ke onaona
I laila ke kaunu ʻana
Kau pono ana nā ka manaʻo.

In Puna's fragrant glades
And ever-present perfume
Passion
Is ever in the thoughts.

*Hui*
Puna paia ʻaʻala
Kilihea i ke onaona
ʻO nawela i ke aloha
Ua lawa iāʻoe me aʻu.

*Chorus*
Puna's fragrant glades
Are drenched with perfume
In a tracery of love
Where you and I suffice.

Hoʻohihi i ka nani
Pua mai a ka lehua.
Ānehe au e kiʻi
I pua kau nō kuʻu umauma.

Entranced with beauty
The *lehua* blossoms.
I come quietly to find
A flower to place upon my heart.

## PŪPŪ O ʻEWA

## SHELLS OF ʻEWA

This rollicking men's song, known also as "Ka-ʻahu-pāhau," honors ʻEwa on Oahu. The composer is not known, but the song is said to have been composed as part of a fund-raising campaign for the Ka-hiku-o-ka-lani Church (the seventh of the kings) at Pearl City. Ka-lā-kaua, the seventh monarch, for whom the church was named, helped build it.

The "news of the land" is the discovery of pearl oysters at Puʻu-loa, the Hawaiian name for Pearl Harbor. Ka-ʻahu-pāhau is the shark goddess who protected Pearl Harbor. Kaʻala, in the Wai-ʻanae range, is the highest mountain on Oahu. Polea is a place at ʻEwa. In

87

the chorus, *nuʻa* and *naue* are sometimes replaced by *nuku* (mouth) and *lawe* (bring).

After being sung for more than a hundred years, an English version called "Pearly Shells" has recently become popular. This is one of the few Hawaiian songs sung successfully in English, but the poetic reference to the shark goddess has not been kept. The music of "Pūpū o ʻEwa" was printed by Smith (1955:vol. 67, no. 2, pp. 18-19, 29).

| *Hui* | *Chorus* |
|---|---|
| Pūpū (aʻo ʻEwa), i ka nuʻa (nā kānaka) | Shells (of ʻEwa), throngs (of people) |
| E naue mai (e ʻike) i ka meahou (o ka ʻāina), | Coming (to learn) the news (of the land), |
| A he ʻāina (ua kaulana), mai nā (kūpuna mai). | A land (famous) from the (ancients on). |
| Alahula Puʻu-loa, he ala hele nō Ka-ʻahu-pāhau (Ka-ʻahu-pāhau). | In the seas of Pearl Harbor, the path trod upon by Ka-ʻahu-pāhau (Ka-ʻahu-pāhau). |
| Alahula Puʻu-loa, he ala hele nō Ka-ʻahu-pāhau (Ka-ʻahu-pāhau). | In the seas of Pearl Harbor, the path trod upon by Ka-ʻahu-pāhau (Ka-ʻahu-pāhau). |
| | |
| Nani Kaʻala, hemolele i ka mālie, | Beautiful Kaʻala, sublime in the calm, |
| Kuahiwi kaulana aʻo ʻEwa, | Famous mountain of ʻEwa |
| E kiʻi ana i ka makani o ka ʻāina. | That fetches the wind of the land. |
| Hea ka Moaʻe, eia au, e ke aloha. | The tradewind calls, here I am, beloved. |
| | |
| Kilakila ʻo Polea noho i ka ʻolu, | Majestic Polea in the coolness, |
| Ia home hoʻohihi a ka malihini, | Home delightful to visitors, |
| E walea ana i ka ʻolu o ke kiawe | Relaxing in the coolness of *kiawe* |
| I ka pā kolonahe a ke Kiu. | And the soft blowing of the Kiu wind. |

## QUEEN'S PRAYER

The words and music were written by Queen Liliʻu-o-ka-lani in March 1895, while she was imprisoned at ʻIo-lani Palace, and it was "lovingly dedicated" to her niece Victoria Ka-ʻiu-lani.

88

'O kou aloha nō
Aia i ka lani,
A 'o kou 'oiā'i'o
Hemolele ho'i.

Your love
Is in heaven,
And your truth
So perfect.

Ko'u noho mihi 'ana
A pa'ahao 'ia,
'O 'oe ku'u lama,
Kou nani, ko'u ko'o.

I live in sorrow
Imprisoned,
You are my light,
Your glory my support.

Mai nānā 'ino'ino
Nā hewa o kānaka,
Akā e huikala
A ma'ema'e nō.

Behold not with malevolence
The sins of man,
But forgive
And cleanse.

Nō laila e ka Haku,
Ma lalo o kou 'ēheu
Kō mākou maluhia
A mau aku nō.

And so, o Lord,
Beneath your wings
Be our peace
Forever more.

## REMEMBER, BE SURE AND BE THERE

Composed by J. Elia. Moa-'ula is a waterfall at Hālawa, Moloka'i.

Pau 'ole ko'u ho'ohihi
I ka wailele o Moa-'ula.
I laila wau la 'ike
I ka wai pā lihi i nā
    pali.

My never ending fascination
In the Moa-'ula waterfall.
There I saw
Water touching lightly upon
    the cliffs.

*Hui*
Aloha ku'u lei pīkake,
Na'u i kiss a ho'omau iho.
E lei nō au i kō aloha.
Remember, be sure and be there.

*Chorus*
Greetings, my *pīkake* lei,
I will kiss you forever.
I am a garland for your love.
Remember, be sure and be there.

'A'ole i pau ka 'i'ini
Ke kuini o nā pua,
Ua hele wale a nohonohea
Lupelupea i ke 'ala.

Desire is never finished
For the queen of flowers,
Lovely
And sweet with fragrance.

## ROYAL HAWAIIAN HOTEL

Composed by Mary Keliiaukai Robins, this song was written in honor of
the present Royal Hawaiian Hotel when it was opened in 1927.

Uluwehiwehi 'oe i ka'u 'ike la,
E ka Royal Hawaiian Hotel.

You are festive to see,
O Royal Hawaiian Hotel.

| *Hui* | *Chorus* |
|---|---|
| A he nani la, ke hulali nei, | Beauty gleaming, |
| A he nani māoli nō. | True beauty. |
| | |
| Ka moena weleweka moe kāua la, | Velvet beds we sleep upon, |
| He pakika he pahe'e maika'i nei. | Smooth, soft and good. |
| | |
| Ka paia māpala 'ōma'oma'o la, | Green marble walls, |
| He pipi'o mau e ke ānuenue. | Rainbow constantly at arch. |
| | |
| 'O ka hone a ke kai i ka pu'u one la | Soft song of sea on sand dunes |
| Me ke 'ala līpoa e moani nei. | Wafting in fragrance of seaweed. |
| | |
| 'O ka holunape a ka lau o ka niu la | Leaves of coconut sway |
| I ke kukulu aumoe. | In the late night. |
| | |
| Ka Hōkū-loa nō kou alaka'i la, | The morning star your guide, |
| 'O ka mana kahikolu kou home. | Power of the trinity your home. |
| | |
| E ō e ka Royal Hawaiian Hotel. | Answer, o Royal Hawaiian Hotel. |
| Kou inoa hanohano ia la. | This is for the glory of your name. |

## SASSY

This song, composed in the 1890's by either J. Kokolia or Solomon Hiram, honors sassy girls in various places, beginning with the then notorious Iwilei district in Honolulu eastward as far as Wai-'alae, mentioning alleged characteristics of each place. This use of place names and descriptive epithets is popular in songs, as in "Hilo Hanakahi" and "Mauna-lua."

| | |
|---|---|
| Kaikamahine nō Iwilei la, | Girl of Iwilei, |
| Sassy ho'i kāu lewa 'ana, | Sassy straying, |
| Ua ma'a wale i ka 'ai 'alamihi la, | Always eating black crabs, |
| Sassy ho'i kāu lewa 'ana. | Sassy straying. |
| | |
| Kaikamahine nō Ka-lihi la, | Girl of Ka-lihi, |
| Sassy ho'i kāu lewa 'ana, | Sassy straying, |
| Ua ma'a wale i ka inu pia la, | Always drinking beer, |
| Sassy ho'i kāu lewa 'ana. | Sassy straying. |
| | |
| Kaikamahine nō Ka-pālama la, | Girl of Ka-pālama, |
| Sassy ho'i kāu lewa 'ana, | Sassy straying, |
| Ua ma'a wale i ka 'ai laiki la, | Always eating rice, |
| Sassy ho'i kāu lewa 'ana. | Sassy straying. |

Kaikamahine nō Kaka'ako la,
Sassy ho'i kāu lewa 'ana,
Aia i ka papa ABC la,
Sassy ho'i kāu lewa 'ana.

Girl of Kaka'ako,
Sassy straying,
There in the ABC class,
Sassy straying.

Wahine haole nō ka Moana
  Hotel,
Sassy ho'i kāu lewa 'ana,
'Elua kālā me ka hapalua la,
Sassy ho'i kāu lewa 'ana.

White woman of the Moana
  Hotel,
Sassy straying,
Two dollars and a half,
Sassy straying.

Kaikamahine nō Wai-kīkī la,
Sassy ho'i kāu lewa 'ana,
Ua ma'a wale i ka 'ai līpoa la,
Sassy ho'i kāu lewa 'ana.

Girl of Waikiki,
Sassy straying,
Always eating seaweed,
Sassy straying.

Kaikamahine nō Wai-'alae la,
Sassy ho'i kāu lewa 'ana,
Ua ma'a wale i ke kau 'ēkake la,
Sassy ho'i kāu lewa 'ana.

Girl of Wai-'alae,
Sassy straying,
Always riding a donkey,
Sassy straying.

Ha'ina 'ia mai ana ka puana la,
Sassy ho'i kāu lewa 'ana,
Ua ma'a wale i ke kau 'ēkake la,
Sassy ho'i kāu lewa 'ana.

Tell the refrain,
Sassy straying,
Always riding a donkey,
Sassy straying.

### SASSY (Maui Version)

Wally Kuloloia, of Makena, Maui, composed the following and kindly
gave permission for its inclusion here.

Keiki kāne nō Mākena la,
Sassy ho'i kāna lewa 'ana,
Ka lawai'a huki lau me ka
  makua la,
Sassy ho'i kāna lewa 'ana.

Boy of Mākena,
Sassy straying,
Fisherman seining with his
    father,
Sassy straying.

Keiki kāne nō 'Ulu-pala-kua la,
Sassy ho'i kāna lewa 'ana,
Ua ma'a wale kau holo lio la,
Sassy ho'i kāna lewa 'ana.

Boy of 'Ulu-pala-kua,
Sassy straying,
Always riding horseback,
Sassy straying.

Keiki kāne nō Hāna la,
Sassy ho'i kāna lewa 'ana,
Ua ma'a wale ku'i poi 'ulu la,
Sassy ho'i kāna lewa 'ana.

Boy of Hāna,
Sassy straying,
Always pounding breadfruit poi,
Sassy straying.

| Kaikamahine nō Pāʻia la, | Girl of Pāʻia, |
|---|---|
| Sassy hoʻi kāna lewa ʻana, | Sassy straying, |
| Ua maʻa wale ka lewa ʻōkole la, | Always swinging hips, |
| Sassy hoʻi kāna lewa ʻana. | Sassy straying. |

| Kaikamahine nō Kahului la, | Girl of Kahului, |
|---|---|
| Sassy hoʻi kāna lewa ʻana, | Sassy straying, |
| Ua maʻa wale i ka hoʻopunipuni la, | Always fibbing, |
| Haʻina ʻia mai ana ka puana la. | Tell the story. |

| Ka lawaiʻa huki lau me ka makua la, | Fisherman seining with his father, |
|---|---|
| Sassy hoʻi kāna lewa ʻana. | Sassy straying. |
| Haʻina ʻia mai ua pau loa la. | The refrain is all *pau*. |

<table>
<tr><th>SWEET LEI MAMO</th><th>SWEET LEI OF SAFFRON FLOWER</th></tr>
</table>

Composed by Huelani.

| Wehiwehi ka uka i ka nahele, | Uplands adorned with growth, |
|---|---|
| Ka popohe lau o ka palai, | Round fern leaves, |
| Hau lipolipo i ke onaona, | Cool fragrance of the depths, |
| Hoa pili o ke ʻaʻaliʻi. | Companion of *ʻaʻaliʻi* tree. |

| *Hui* | *Chorus* |
|---|---|
| Sweet lei mamo (mamo), | Sweet lei *mamo*, |
| Lei o ke aloha (loha), | Lei of love, |
| Kāhiko nani oʻu, | My beautiful adornment, |
| Sweet lei mamo (mamo). | Sweet lei *mamo*. |

| Ka uhi paʻa ka noe, | Covered with mist, |
|---|---|
| Ka luna ʻolu o Kilohana, | Cool summit of Kilohana, |
| I laila hoʻi au i ʻike ai | There I saw |
| Kahi wai huʻi o Lei-aloha. | Cool waters of Lei-aloha. |

| Honehone leo o ke kāhuli, | Soft voice of land shell, |
|---|---|
| Leo leʻa o ka wao kele, | Happy voice of the deep forest, |
| Ka ʻiʻiwi ka hoa e like ai, | The *ʻiʻiwi* bird, too, is a friend, |
| My sweet lei mamo. | My sweet lei *mamo*. |

<table>
<tr><th>TŪTŪ</th><th>GRANNY</th></tr>
</table>

This hula was composed by Queen Liliʻu-o-ka-lani for a benefit for Kau-maka-pili Church in Pā-lama, Honolulu. Maira Heleluhe took the role of *tūtū* and seven little girls, all uniformly dressed, acted as grandchildren. The queen trained the girls to sing this song and accompanied them on her guitar, singing with them. The song was a great success, and lots of nickels, dimes, and quarters were showered on the singers. One little girl was so tired of singing that she cried after five encores and they had to stop singing. Afterwards all the singers were called *tūtū* by their friends.

Ka'ala'ala'a is near Nu'u-anu below Ma'ema'e hill.

Aia i Ka'ala'ala'a
Ku'u wahi kupuna wahine,
Ua nui kona mau lā
'O ka noho 'ana i ke ao nei.

There at Ka'ala'ala'a
My little grandmother,
Many are her days
Living in this world.

Kāna hana i ke kakahiaka
'O ka wehe i ka Paipala nui,
Ki'i aku la i nā maka aniani
A penei e kau ai.

Her first act in the morning
To open the big Bible,
Get her glasses
And put them on this way.

*Hui*
E aloha kākou iāia,
E mālama kākou ia Tūtū,
E ho'āno kākou iāia,
Kō kākou kupuna wahine.

*Chorus*
We love her,
We care for *Tūtū*,
We honor her,
Our grandmother.

A kau mai i ke ahiahi
Ho'omākaukau e pule
Ki'i aku la i nā maka aniani,
Auwē! ua nalowale.

When evening comes
Preparing for devotion
Looking for her glasses,
*Auwē!* disappeared.

Aia i ka lae,
I ka lae kahi kau ai,
Ua poina loa 'ia
I luna i ka lae.

There on her forehead,
Placed on her forehead,
Quite forgotten
High on her forehead.

## WAI O KE ANIANI

## CRYSTAL WATER

The old name of this song was "Wai Hu'ihu'i o ke Aniani." Kā'ili-kahi was the name of a *heiau* at Kaha-lu'u, Oahu.

Nani nō ke 'ala
Ke 'ala o ka pua pīkake
'O ka noe a ka ua li'ili'i,
Ka 'uhene a ka wai i ka
'ili.

Beautiful is the scent
Scent of *pīkake* flowers
In mist of fine rain,
In the happy sound of water over stones.

|                             |                             |
| --------------------------- | --------------------------- |
| *Hui*                       | *Chorus*                    |
| Huʻi au konikoni            | Cold am I and tingling      |
| I ka wai konikoni,          | In tingling water,          |
| Wai huʻihuʻi o ke aniani.   | Cool, crystal water.        |
|                             |                             |
| ʻO ka noe a ka ua liʻiliʻi, | In mist of fine rain,       |
| I ka uka o Kāʻili-kahi,     | Inland at Kāʻili-kahi,      |
| Hoʻokahi pua nani o ka liko,| The most beautiful flower bud,|
| Ka ʻōnohi wai ānuenue.      | A patch of rainbow water.   |

An alternate first stanza has the following first two lines:

|                             |                             |
| --------------------------- | --------------------------- |
| Ua laʻi nō ke ʻala          | Peaceful is the fragrance   |
| I ka liko o ka pua pīkake.  | Of *pīkake* flower buds.    |


### WAI-PIʻO

This song was probably written in the 1860's. It is a woman's praise of her isolated home at Wai-piʻo, Hawaiʻi, its beautiful waterfall called Hiʻilawe, her relatives, friends, and neighbors, and her half-Spanish lover. She defies the gossips who have compared her to King Herod of the Bible. In the fifth stanza are two sayings: "The fish caught in the hands" is probably a lover; "Wai-piʻo is drowsy in the mist" is a poetical expression for one who has had much to drink; here it means that the singer's happiness is so great that she is indifferent to her isolation and the unkind remarks of others. See "Hiʻilawe" for another song about an adventurous woman at the same place.

|                             |                             |
| --------------------------- | --------------------------- |
| Kaulana kuʻu home puni      | Famous is my home, beloved  |
| Wai-piʻo,                   | Wai-piʻo,                   |
| Me nā peʻa nani o ka        | And the beautiful fringes of the |
| ʻāina.                      | land.                       |
| Kākela he hale aliʻi,       | A castle, a royal residence,|
| Herode koʻu hoa            | Yet I (am said to be) like my |
| like,                       | friend Herod,               |
| Mōʻī puni haʻakei.          | King with evil pride.       |
|                             |                             |
| Kukuna o ka lā koʻu kapa ia | My garments are rays of the sun |
| E ʻōlino nei a puni ka honua,| Sparkling on all the land,  |
| Auwē aʻe luna lilo          | But far, far away           |
| Lihi launa ʻole mai         | And never to be             |
| Nā aliʻi nui o ke ao.       | With great persons of the world.|

94

E o'u mau kini nā makamaka,
Me nā kupa o ku'u 'āina,
Me ka wailele a'o Hi'ilawe
Ko'iawe maila i luna,
Ko'iawe mau i ka pali.

'A'ole pēlā ka 'oiā'i'o,
Haku 'epa loko 'ino a ka
    makamaka,
Ua like nō a like
Me nā kini lehulehu
O ku'u one hānau.

E ola māua me a'u kini,
Me a'u lei o nei
    'āina
Pulupē i ka hunakai,
Ka i'a mili i ka
    lima.
Heha Wai-pi'o i ka noe.

Ha'ina 'ia mai ana ka puana:
Nō ka lei hapa pua Sepania,
He kupa nō ka 'āina,
E kipa mai maloko,
Hale-'iwa beautiful home.

My only relatives and friends,
Old natives of my land,
The waterfall of Hi'ilawe
Gushing down from above,
Gushing always on the cliff.

Not thus the truth,
Just wicked lies of
    friends,
And also
Of the crowds
On the sands of my birth.

He and I and my relatives,
And my children stay in this
    land
Drenched with sea spray,
Where fish are caught in the
    hands.
Wai-pi'o is drowsy in the mist.

Tell the refrain:
Half-Spanish flower lei,
Old native of the land,
Visiting within,
Hale-'iwa beautiful home.

## WEHIWEHI
## 'OE

## YOU ARE SO
## DECORATIVE

Composed by Sylvester Ka-lama.

E ku'u pua mae
    'ole
A'u i kui ai a
    lawa.
I lei ho'ohiehie
Nō ke ano ahiahi.
            *Hui*
Wehiwehi 'oe, e ku'u
    ipo,
He 'i'ini ke ko'i'i waiho
    iā loko
'O loko hana nui i ka
    pu'uwai
Kō leo nahenahe e maliu mai.

O flower of mine that never
    fades
That I wear as a lei bound
    strongly.
You are so elegant
In the evening.
            *Chorus*
You are so decorative, my
    sweetheart,
And you evoke within desire so
    persistent
That it is impossible for the
    heart
Not to heed your soft voice.

Hoʻohihi ka manaʻo aʻe ʻike
I ka lau ʻāhihi o ia uka
I puia i ke ʻala
   onaona
Me ka ua hāliʻi i ka
   nahele.

One wants to know and love
The creeping vines of the uplands
Drenched with fragrance and
   perfume
And the rain spread through the
   forest.

# CHRISTMAS SONGS

These songs were adapted from English and the words were tailored to fit the music. They were meant to be sung in Hawaii, and therefore certain changes were made in the originals. In this book they have been translated from the Hawaiian back into English so that singers not very familiar with Hawaiian will know the meaning of the content words.

## AULD LANG SYNE

The following are three Hawaiian translations of this famous song. The first is by Lili'u-o-ka-lani. The solos in this version use the singular *ke hoa* (the friend) and the dual *kāua* (you and I). The choruses use the plural *nā hoa* (the friends) and *kākou* (all of us). The second and third versions were published in the *Paradise of the Pacific* (December 1891), and in *Ka Nupepa Kuokoa* (September 16, 1893). The 1891 variant is more literal and more difficult to sing.

### Lili'u-o-ka-lani Version

E poina 'ia anei ke hoa / Is the friend forgotten
'A'ole e ho'omana'o? / And not remembered?
E poina 'ia anei ke hoa / Is the friend forgotten
O nā lā i 'aui a'e? / Of days long past?

*Hui* / *Chorus*

E poina 'ia anei nā hoa / Are the friends forgotten
O nā lā o ka makali'i? / Of the days of the summer months?
E mau ka ho'omana'o 'ana / Keep the memory
Nō nā lā i 'aui a'e. / Of days long past.

Kāua ka i alo i ka nahele / You and I go to the forest
A 'ako i nā pua kamaha'o. / And pick astonishing flowers.
Kāua pū ka i 'ike i ka luhi / Only you and I know the burdens
I nä lā i hala 'ē aku. / Of days long gone.

*Hui* / *Chorus*

Kākou ka i alo i ka nahele / All of us go to the forest
A 'ako i nā pua kamaha'o. / And pick astonishing flowers.
Kākou ka i 'ike pū i ka luhi / We all know the burdens
I nā lā i 'aui a'e. / Of days long past.

Eia mai e aloha, e ka hoa, / Greetings, o friend,
Huli mai kākou i 'ane'i / Let us come here
A 'e hui me ka ho'omana'o / And unite in memory
I nā lā i 'aui a'e. / Of days long past.

98

Nō ke aha la nā hoaloha kahiko
i poina ai
A hoʻomanaʻo ʻole kahi i
kekahi?
Nō ke aha la nā hoaloha kahiko
i poina ai
O nā lā lōʻihi i hala?

*Hui*

A nō laila nō ka manawa i
hala kuʻu hoalauna
Nō ka manawa lōʻihi i hala,
Aʻe lawe kāua i ke kīʻaha o
ke aloha
Nō ka manawa lōʻihi i hala.

Kāua ʻelua ka i hele ma nā pali
A ʻako hoʻi i nā pua o puʻu
nani
Akā, ua ʻauwana kāua ma nā
wahi lehulehu
Mahope mai o kēlā manawa i hala.

Kāua ʻelua ka i ʻauʻau i loko
o ke kahawai
Mai ke kakahiaka a hiki i ke
awakea ʻana
Akā, nā ka moana ākea i
hoʻoka ʻawale ʻia kāua
Mahope mai o kēlā manawa i
hala.

Eia kuʻu lima, e kuʻu hoaloha
ʻoiāʻiʻo,
Aʻe hāʻawi mai hoʻi ʻoe i
kou lima,
Aʻe lawe kāua i ka inu maikaʻi
ʻana
Nō ka manawa lōʻihi i hala.

A nō ka ʻoiāʻiʻo, e lawe mai ʻoe
i kou kīʻaha
A pēlā hoʻi au i koʻu.
Aʻe lawe kāua i ke kīʻaha o
ke aloha
Nō ka manawa lōʻihi i hala.

Why should old friends
forget
And one remember not the
other?
Why should old friends
forget
Days long past?

*Chorus*

So old neighbors of past
times
Times long past,
Let's lift a cup of
kindness
To times long past.

We went to the cliffs
And picked flowers of the pretty
hills
And we wandered in many
places
After that past time.

We swam in the
streams
From morning to
afternoon
And by the wide ocean we were
separated
After that past
time.

Here is my hand, true
friend,
And give me too your
hand,
Let's take good
drinks
To days long past.

And in truth bring your
glass
And so I will mine.
Let's lift a cup of
kindness
To times long past.

| | |
|---|---|
| Poina anei ka hoa o'u | Do my friends forget |
| A nalo loa nō? | And lose forever? |
| Poina anei ka hoa o'u | Do my friends forget |
| Nā la'i, nā la'i nei? | Peace, this peace? |

| *Hui* | *Chorus* |
|---|---|
| E ho'omana'o nā lā a pau | Remember every day |
| I launa aloha pū, | To gather with aloha, |
| E lūlū lima aloha nō | To shake hands with aloha |
| Ka hoa aloha o'u. | My beloved friends. |

## BETELEHEMA IKI Ē

## O LITTLE TOWN OF BETHLEHEM

Translated by Edward Ka-hale.

| Betelehema iki ē, | Little Bethlehem, |
|---|---|
| Ke 'ike nei mākou | We see |
| Kou moe 'ana i ka pō, | Your sleep at night, |
| Pane'e a'e nā hōkū | The stars advance |
| La'ela'e nō kou mau ala, | Bright for your pathway, |
| Ka lama e ola ai, | Light of salvation, |
| Ka li'a, ka weli o nā kau | The yearning and awe of the seasons |
| Aia nō me 'oe. | Are with you. |

| Hānau 'ia 'o Kristo | Christ is born |
|---|---|
| A hui a'e kō 'ō. | Meeting there. |
| Moe kō ke ao a kia'i mau, | The world sleeps guarded ever, |
| Nā 'ānela maika'i | Good angels |
| Hui pū nā hōkū ao. | Meeting the stars of dawn. |
| Kūkala a'e 'oukou | You proclaim |
| A mililani i ke Akua | Praise of God |
| He malu i kānaka. | And peace to man. |

## DECK THE HALLS

This song was translated by Mary Kawena Pukui in July 1968. Each *la* is repeated eight times.

| Ho'onani i ka hale — la | Deck the halls — la |
|---|---|
| He manawa ho'ohau'oli — la | A time to make merry — la |
| Komo i nā 'ahu nani — la | Put on fine clothes — la |
| E mele nō ka lā Kalikimaka — la. | And sing for Christmas day — la. |

100

A ke ahi mālamalama — la
Kani mai nā pila 'oli — la
A hulahula hau'oli a'e — la
Hō'ike nō ka lā Kalikimaka — la.

The bright fire — la
Fiddles play with joy — la
For happy dancing — la
Signs of Christmas day — la.

Hala a'e ia makahiki — la
E hau'oli i ka mea hou — la
Mele 'oli pū kākou — la
'A'ohe hopo i ke ko'eko'e — la.

The year has gone — la
Be happy for the new — la
Let us sing together — la
And not fear cold — la.

## E HELE MAI 'OUKOU KA PO'E MANA'O'I'O

## O COME ALL YE FAITHFUL

E hele mai 'oukou, ka po'e
   mana'o'i'o,
E hele hau'oli i Betelehema,
Hele mai a 'ike i ka Mō'ī
   hānau hou.

Come, faithful
   people,
Go happily to Bethlehem,
Come and see the new-born
   King.

Ka lama i 'ō mai ka lani mai.
Nani ka hua a ka
   Virgine,
Akua maoli i hana 'ole 'ia.

The torch there from heaven.
Beautiful is the child of
   the Virgin,
True God, not graven.

*Hui*
Ho'onani kākou iā Ia,
Ho'onani kākou iā Ia,
Ho'onani kākou iā Ia,
Kristo ka Haku.

*Chorus*
Let us adore Him,
Let us adore Him,
Let us adore Him,
Christ the Lord.

## HĀMAU 'E NĀ KĀNAKA

## HARK! THE HERALD ANGELS SING

Hāmau 'e nā kānaka,
Mele mai nā 'ānela,
Eia ke Li'i hānau hou,
E ho'onani (a'e) 'oukou!
Malu nō kō lalo nei
E hau'oli ho'omaika'i!
Ke Akua kō ke ao,
Ku'ikahi pū lākou.
Ke Akua kō ke ao,
Ku'ikahi pū lākou.

Silence, O people,
The angels sing,
Here is the new-born Chief,
Sing praises!
Here below is so peaceful
Rejoice congratulate!
The God of the world,
They are united.
The God of the world,
They are united.

Oli (a'e) nā 'āina a pau,
Oli pū me kēlā ao.

All the lands sing chants,
Chant together with the world.

E haʻi aʻe mai ʻō a ʻō,
ʻIesū ke Liʻi nō kākou,
Hele mai ka lani mai,
Hānau ʻia nō maʻaneʻi,
Nō kākou i hānau hou,
A loaʻa ke ola mau.
Nō kākou i hānau hou,
A loaʻa ke ola mau.

Saying here and there,
Jesus the Chief for us,
Come from heaven,
Born for us,
Born again for us,
To gain eternal life.
Born again for us,
To gain eternal life.

E aloha ke Liʻi mau,
Ke Liʻi pono nō kākou.
Lama ola malu nō,
Nō keia ao a pau.
Mele ʻē nā kānaka,
Mele me nā ʻānela,
Eia ke Liʻi hānau hou,
Pōmaikaʻi a malu mau.
Eia ke Liʻi hānau hou,
Pōmaikaʻi a malu mau.

Hail eternal Chief,
The Chief for us.
Torch [of] peaceful life,
For all this world.
Sing before, people,
Sing with the angels,
Here is the new-born Chief,
Blessings and eternal peace.
Here is the new-born Chief,
Blessings and eternal peace.

## HE PŌ LAʻELAʻE

## IT CAME UPON THE MIDNIGHT CLEAR

Translated by Edward Ka-hale.

Ka pō laʻelaʻe ka hikina mai,
    i mele ʻoli nei
Mai nā ʻānela i ke ao, hoʻokani
    mai lākou
He malu he aloha nō, mai ka
    Makua mai,
Mehameha ke ao a pau, aloha
    nō lākou.

In the clear night comes this
    joyous song
From the angels in the air they
    sing
Of peace, of love from the
    Lord,
Silence in all the world, they
    love.

Mai loko mai o ke ao, a wehe
    aʻe nā ʻeheu
A ʻo nā mele ke ʻō mai la, i ke
    ao luhi nei.
Maluna aʻe o ka honua, kūlou
    mai nō lākou.
Hoʻokani nō a lohe ʻia ka leo
    o nā ʻānela.

Within in the air, opening
    wings
The songs that endure in this
    tired world.
Above the earth they
    bow.
Sing and listen to the voices
    of the angels.

## KANA KALOKA

Composed by Mary Kawena Pukui in the early 1950's.

Hiki mai 'o Kana Kaloka
Mai ka 'āina hau anu,
Lele mai i Hawai'i
Me nā kia punahele.

*Hui*
Kani mai nā pele e,
Kani 'oli, kanikē,
Kani mai nā pele e
Mele Kalikimaka.

He mau maka 'olu'olu,
'Umi'umi pūhuluhulu,
Pa'alole 'ula'ula,
'Oia nō 'o Kana Kaloka.

He 'eke nui kāna
Piha pono i nā makana
He mea ho'ohau'oli
Iā kākou nō apau.

## KANI NĀ PELE

Translated by Ronald Brown.

Kani nā pele,
Kani nā pele,
Kani nā wā apau.
Le'ale'a nō ke kau 'oe
Ma ke ka'a holo
    hau.

Hā'ule mai ka hau
A holo nō lākou
Maluna o nā kula
Me nā leo hau'oli.

Kani mai nā pele,
Hau'oli nui nō,
Ka hele 'ana i ka holo
Hau keia pō.

## SANTA CLAUS

Santa Claus comes
From the land of cold and snow,
Flies here to Hawaii
With favorite deer.

*Chorus*
Bells ring,
Ring with joy, ring dingdong,
Bells ring
Merry Christmas.

Kind eyes,
Shaggy beard,
Red uniform,
This is Santa Claus.

He has a big bag
Full of gifts
To bring joy
To all of us.

## JINGLE BELLS

The bells ring,
The bells ring,
Ring all the time.
Happy when you ride
On the vehicle running on
    the snow.

The snow falls
They ride
On the plains
With happy voices.

The bells ring,
So very happy,
To go riding
On the snow tonight.

# LITTLE DRUMMER BOY

Translated by Mary Kawena Pukui in August 1968. The chorus is similar in each stanza.

| | |
|---|---|
| Kono 'ia mai au, pa rum pum<br>    pum pum<br>E 'ike i ke li'i, pa rum pum<br>    pum pum<br>Me nā makana nāna, rum pum<br>    pum pum<br>E waiho i ke alo, rum pum pum<br>    pum, rum pum pum pum,<br>    rum pum pum pum<br>E ho'ohanohano, pa rum pum<br>    pum pum<br>Ke hiki aku. | I am invited, pa rum pum<br>    pum pum<br>To see the chief, pa rum pum<br>    pum pum<br>With gifts for him, rum pum<br>    pum pum<br>To leave before him, rum pum<br>    pum pum, rum pum pum<br>    pum, rum pum pum pum<br>To honor, pa rum pum<br>    pum pum<br>His coming. |
| E ke ali'i Iesū,<br>He kama hune au,<br>'A'ohe a'u makana<br>Kūpono na ke ali'i,<br>E ho'okani aku au<br>I ku'u pahu nei. | O Jesus chief,<br>I am a little child,<br>I have no gifts<br>Fit for the chief,<br>I play<br>My drum. |
| Kūnou 'o Malia,<br>'Oli'oli nā holoholona<br>Ho'okani au i ku'u pahu<br>Me ka ho'omaika'i.<br>Mino'aka mai ia<br>Ia'u nei. | Mary bows,<br>Animals rejoice,<br>I play my drum<br>With thanksgiving.<br>She smiles<br>At me. |

## MELE KALIKIMAKA IĀ KĀKOU / MERRY CHRISTMAS FOR US

| | |
|---|---|
| Mele Kalikimaka iā kākou<br>I nēia lā hau'oli,<br>Lā hānau o ka Haku,<br>Keiki hiwahiwa a ke Akua. | Merry Christmas for us<br>This happy day,<br>Birthday of the Lord,<br>Holy child of God. |
| Mele Kalikimaka iā kākou<br>I nēia lā hau'oli,<br>Lā hānau o ka Haku,<br>Keiki a ke Akua. | Merry Christmas for us<br>This happy day,<br>Birthday of the Lord,<br>Child of God. |

104

Hānau ʻia ʻo Iesū
Ma Betelehema o Iudea
I ke kau o Herode,
Ke aliʻi o ʻAikupita.

Jesus was born
In Bethlehem in Judea
At the time of Herod,
King of Egypt.

## PŌ LAʻI Ē

## SILENT NIGHT

Translated by Stephen and Mary Desha.

Pō laʻi ē, pō kamahaʻo,
Maluhia, mālamalama,
Ka makuahine aloha ē
Me ke keiki hemolele ē
Moe me ka maluhia lani.
Moe me ka maluhia lani.

Peaceful night, wonderful night,
Peace, light,
The beloved mother
With the holy child
Sleep in heavenly peace.
Sleep in heavenly peace.

Pō laʻi ē, pō kamahaʻo,
Oni nā kahu hipa ē
I kō ka lani nani nō.
Mele nā ʻānela haleluia.
Hānau ʻia Kristo ka haku.
Hānau ʻia Kristo ka haku.

Peaceful night, wonderful night,
The shepherds come
With the heavenʻs beauty.
The angels sing hallelujah.
Christ the Lord is born.
Christ the Lord is born.

Pō laʻi ē, pō kamahaʻo,
Keiki hiwahiwa aloha ē,
Ka lama laʻi mai luna mai
Me ka lokomaikaʻi makamae.
Iesū i kou hānau ʻana.
Iesū i kou hānau ʻana.

Peaceful night, wonderful night,
Beloved sacred child,
Light of peace from above
With goodwill and purity.
Jesus for your birth.
Jesus for your birth.

## PŌMAIKAʻI WALE
## KŌ KE AO

## JOY TO THE
## WORLD

Composed by Hiram Bingham, the leading member of the First
Company of Missionaries (1820) who was more noted for sternness
than for joy. He dominated the mission for twenty years.

Pōmaikaʻi wale kō ke ao,
Ua hiki mai ke Aliʻi.
E moe, e nā ʻāina a pau,
E malu nui mai,
E malu nui mai,
E malu, malu nui mai.

Blessings of the world,
The Chief has come.
Sleep, O lands all,
Great peace has come,
Great peace has come,
Peace, great peace has come.

Hauʻoli ʻo Iesū ke Aliʻi,
Mahalo kānaka.
Hoʻokani aʻe nā mea a pau

Joy, Jesus is the Chief,
Men give thanks.
All persons sing

E pau ho'i nā kīnā,
E pau ho'i na kīnā,
E pau, e pau ho'i nā kīnā.

Mai ulu wale hou ma'ane'i
Nā 'ino nō ka pō.
Nā Iesū i hā'awi mai
Ka maika'i wale nō,
Ka maika'i wale nō,
Ka maika'i, maika'i wale nō.

A nāna e ho'omalu mau
Ke aupuni pōmaika'i.
A 'ike pū nā 'āina a pau
Ia pono e ola ai,
Ia pono e ola ai,
Ia pono, pono e ola
    ai.

Blemishes are gone,
Blemishes are gone,
Gone, blemishes are gone.

No longer will here arise
The sins of ignorance.
Jesus has given
Goodness only,
Goodness only,
Goodness, goodness only.

He will always protect
The blessed kingdom.
All lands will see
This righteousness of salvation,
This righteousness of salvation,
This righteousness, righteousness
    of salvation.

# REFERENCES

Alexander, W. D. 1864. *A Short Synopsis of the Most Essential Points in Hawaiian Grammar.*

Andrews, Lorrin. 1875. "Remarks on Hawaiian Poetry," *The Islander,* 1:26, 27, 30, 31, 35.

Beckwith, Martha Warren. 1919. "The Hawaiian Romance of Laieikawai (by S. N. Haleole, 1863) with Introduction and Translation." Bureau of American Ethnology, Annual Reports, No. 33:285-677.

————— 1951. *The Kumulipo, a Hawaiian Creation Chant.* Chicago: University of Chicago Press.

Caldwell, Helen. 1915. "Hawaiian Music," *Hawaiian Almanac and Annual for 1916:*71-79.

Colum, Padraic. 1924. "A Note on Hawaiian Poetry." *The Dial,* April.

Damon, Ethel M. 1957. *Sanford Ballard Dole and His Hawaii.* Palo Alto: Pacific Books.

Elbert, Samuel H. (ed.). 1959. *Selections from Fornander's Hawaiian Antiquities and Folk-lore.* Honolulu: University of Hawaii Press.

————— 1962. "Symbolism in Hawaiian Poetry," *ETC.: A Review of General Semantics,* XVIII:389-400.

Ellis, William. 1963. *Narrative of a Tour of Hawaii.* Honolulu: Advertiser Publishing Co. (revision of an 1826 publication).

Emerson, Nathaniel B. 1909. *Unwritten Literature of Hawaii, the Sacred Songs of the Hula, Collected and Translated, with Notes and an Account of the Hula.* Bureau of American Ethnology Bulletins, No. 38.

————— 1915. *Pele and Hiiaka, a Myth from Hawaii.* Honolulu.

————— 1965. *Unwritten Literature of Hawaii, the Sacred Songs of the Hula.* Rutland and Tokyo: Charles E. Tuttle Co. (reprint of a 1909 publication).

Fornander, Abraham. 1916-1919. *Fornander Collection of Hawaiian Antiquities and Folk-Lore.* Honolulu: Bernice P. Bishop Museum Memoirs, volumes 4-6.

Kamakau, S. M. 1961. *Ruling Chiefs of Hawaii.* Honolulu: Kamehameha Schools Press.

Kuykendall, Ralph S. 1967. *The Hawaiian Kingdom, 1874-1893.* Honolulu: University of Hawaii Press.

Liliuokalani. 1897. "He Buke Mele Hawaii i Haku Ponoi, Hoonohonoho a Mahele Ia a Liliuokalani o Hawaii. He Mea Hoonanea no ka La Walea, Wakine-kona, Mokuaina o Kolumepia," (A Book of Hawaiian Songs Composed Personally, Arranged and Divided by Liliuokalani of Hawaii. A Pastime for Leisure Days, Washington, District of Columbia). Unpublished manuscript, State of Hawaii Archives.

————— 1898. *Hawaii's Story by Hawaii's Queen.* Boston.

*Lira Kamalii, Oia na Himeni Haipule me na Himeni Wale, Pai Pu me na Mele, no na Kamalii Hawaii* (Children's Lyrics, Religious Hymns and Recreational

Songs, Published Together with Songs for Hawaiian Children). N.d. New York: American Tract Society.

Luther, Frank. 1940. "Americans and Their Songs." In: University of Missouri Studies *Ballads and Songs,* 15:48-49.

Na Mele Hoonanea ("Recreational Songs"). N.d.

Plews, Edith Rice. 1968. "Poetry." *Ancient Hawaiian Civilization, a Series of Lectures Delivered at the Kamehameha Schools.* Revised edition. Rutland and Tokyo: Charles E. Tuttle Co., pp. 173-197. (The first edition was published in 1933.)

Pukui, Mary Kawena. 1949. "Songs (Meles) of Old Kaʻu, Hawaii," *Journal of American Folklore,* July-September: 247-258.

———— and Samuel H. Elbert. 1964. *English-Hawaiian Dictionary.* Honolulu: University of Hawaii Press.

———— ———— 1965. *Hawaiian-English Dictionary.* Third edition. Honolulu: University of Hawaii Press.

———— ———— 1966. *Place Names of Hawaii.* Honolulu: University of Hawaii Press.

Rice, William Hyde. 1923. *Hawaiian Legends.* Honolulu: B. P. Bishop Museum Bulletin 3.

Roberts, Helen H. 1926. *Ancient Hawaiian Music.* Honolulu: B. P. Bishop Museum Bulletin 29.

Sapir, Edward. 1939. *Language: An Introduction to the Study of Speech.* New York.

Smith, Barbara B. 1959. "Folk Music in Hawaii," *Journal of the International Folk Music Council,* 11:50-55.

Smith, Emerson C. 1955. "Know Hawaii's Songs," *Paradise of the Pacific,* 67 (2):18-19, 28-29; (3):18-19, 22; (4):14-15, 26; (5):14-15, 26; (9):26, 29.

Topham, Helen A. 1955. "The Function of the Chant in the Legend of Kawelo," *Journal of Oriental Literature,* VI (2):24-31.

Winne, Jane Lathrop. 1968. "Music." *Ancient Hawaiian Civilization, a Series of Lectures Delivered at the Kamehameha Schools.* Revised edition. Rutland and Tokyo: Charles E. Tuttle Co., pp. 199-211. (The first edition was published in 1933.)

# APPENDIX: COMPOSERS

Ae'a: "Hilo March," "Ho'oheno"

Alohikea: "Hanohano Hanalei," "Ka Ua Loku," "Pua Lilia"

Beckley: "Ahi Wela"

Berger: "Beautiful 'Ilima," "Hawai'i Pono'ī," "Hilo March"

Bingham: "Pōmaika'i Kō ke Ao"

Brown: "Kani nā Pele"

De Fries: "Beautiful 'Ilima"

Desha: "Pō La'i ē"

Doirin: "Ahi Wela"

Elia: "Hālona," "Remember Be Sure and Be There"

Ha'i: " 'Ahulili"

Heleluhe: "Ho'oheno"

Hiram: "Ka Moa'e," "Sassy" (?)

Holt: "Makalapua"

Hopkins: "Ku'u Home o nā Pali Hāuliuli"

Huelani: "Sweet Lei Mamo"

Ka'apa: " 'Ālika"

Ka-hale: "Betelehema Iki ē," "He Pō La'ela'e"

Ka-hinu: "Nā Hala o Naue"

Ka-lā-kaua: "Hawai'i Pono'ī," "Koni Au i ka Wai"

Ka-lama: "Wehiwehi 'Oe"

Kāne: "Ka Makani Kā'ili Aloha," "Moloka'i Nui a Hina"

Ka-pa'akea: "Maika'i Kaua'i"

Kauila: "Nā 'Ono o ka 'Āina"

Ke-'alaka'i: "Lei 'Awapuhi"

Kinney: "Holoholo Ka'a"

Kokolio: "Sassy" (?)

Kuloloia: "Sassy"

Konia: "Makalapua"

Kong: "Kāne'ohe"

Kuahiwi: "Na Āli'i"

Kuakini: "Hi'ilawe"

Lele-iō-Hoku: "Adios ke Aloha," "Hole Wai-mea," "Kāua i ka Huahua'i," "Ke Ka'upu"

Likelike: " 'Āina-hau," "Ku'u Ipo i ka He'e Pu'e One"

Lili'u-o-ka-lani: "Aloha 'Oe," "He Inoa nō Ka'iu-lani," "He Kanikau nō Lele-io-Hoku," "He Mele Lāhui Hawai'i," "Ka Wiliwiliwai," "Kokohi," "Ku'u Pua i Paoa-ka-lani," "Puia ka Nahele," "Puna Paia 'A'ala," "Queen's Prayer," "Tūtū," "Auld Lang Syne"

Luna-lilo: "Alekoki"

Lyons: "Hawai'i Aloha"

Montano: "Old Plantation"

Mossman: "Hele Au i Kaleponi," "He 'Ono," "Niu Haohao"

Nā-hinu: "Iā 'Oe e ka Lā"

Nape: "Moana-lua," "Old Plantation"

Nā-wāhine: " 'Ekolu Mea Nui"

Noble: "Kāne-'ohe," "Lāna'i,"

Parker: "Hawaiian Rough Riders"

Prendergast: "Kaulana nā Pua"

Pukui: "Ke Ao Nani," "Ku'u Lei," "Ku'u Lei Pūpū," "Deck the Halls," "Kana Kaloka," "Little Drummer Boy"

Robins: "Lāna'i," "Royal Hawaiian Hotel"

Waia'u: "Ka-'ili-lau-o-ke-koa," "Maika'i Kaua'i"

Wilcox: "Kamuela King"

Wong: " 'Ālika Spoehr Hula"